CARL GARDNER is thirty-eight years old and has been a regular visitor to Paris since he was fourteen. He was TV columnist on *Time Out* from 1978 to 1981 and on *City Limits* from 1981 to 1982. He has also worked in television, on Channel 4's *Voices* series, and as a freelance editor and journalist for such publications as *Radio Times*, the *Observer* and *London Food News*. He is currently assistant editor of *Design* magazine.

JULIE SHEPPARD is thirty-five years old and has worked on a major TV series about food (*Food for Thought*). She has written numerous reports and articles about food and health and currently works for the London Food Commission.

Carl Gardner & Julie Sheppard

Eating PARIS

*A guide
to moderately priced
eating in Paris*

100 restaurants reviewed

PLUS

100 wine-bars, cafés and food-shops

Fontana/Collins

First published in 1987 by Fontana Paperbacks,
8 Grafton Street, London W1X 3LA

Drawings by Ray Evans
Maps by RDL Artset

Made and printed in Great Britain by
William Collins Sons & Co Ltd, Glasgow

Contents

ACKNOWLEDGEMENTS

This book is a distillation of wisdom from a range of sources both written and spoken. In particular we would like to thank Sharon Kivland for helpful suggestions; Nicole Chartier and Charlotte Warzager for advice and accommodation; Marilyn and 'Reif' ('desserts are where it's at') Reifner for moral support in eating our way round Paris; Muriel Sheppard for help with the word-processing; Michael Fishwick at Fontana for his help and encouragement; and all the other people in Britain and France who have given us suggestions and useful criticism.

We would like to dedicate the book to our dear friend and *routard extraordinaire*, Pierre Josse, who has undoubtedly been our biggest influence, guide and support.

MAPS OF PARIS

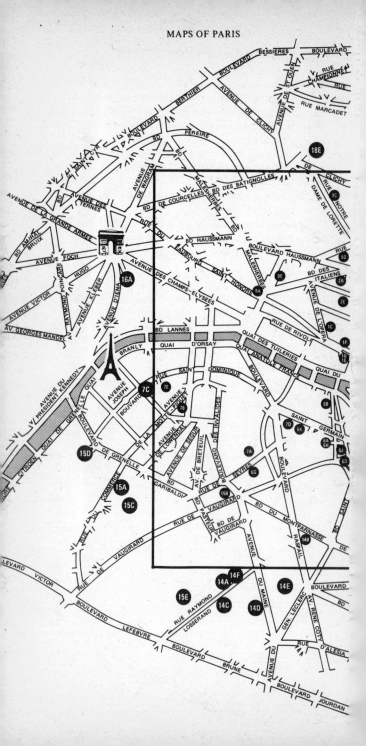

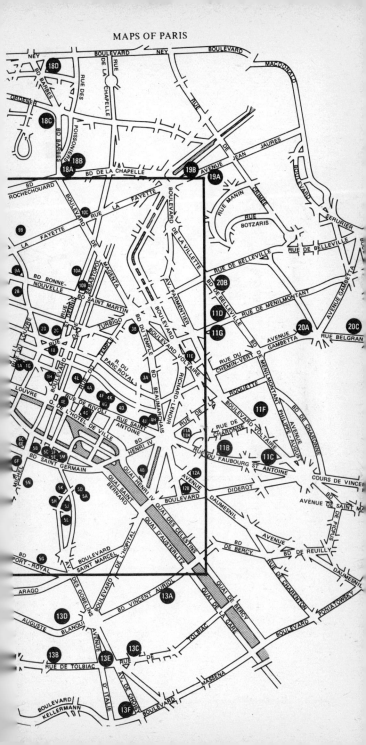

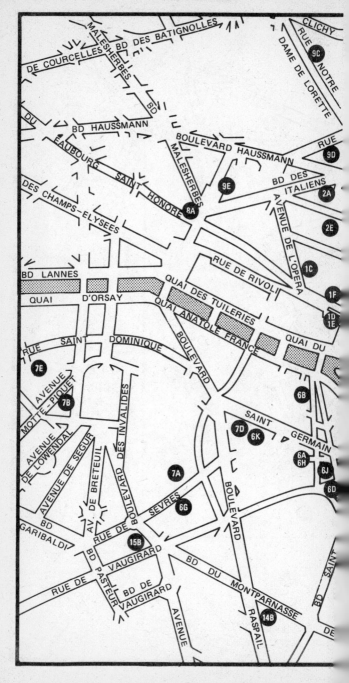

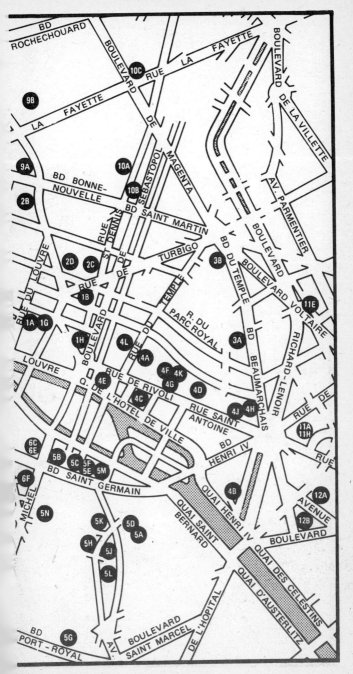

Introduction

Paris has a reputation for being the gastronomic capital of the world, where food is taken most seriously and where it is possible to eat the most wonderful food imaginable. Some of this reputation is well deserved, but increasingly even Parisians admit that eating out in Paris is not what it used to be. The decline of the family-owned establishment, an increase in the use of processed foods and the growth of tourism have all contributed to a deterioration in standards. Such is now the gap between reputation and reality that many visitors to the city, expecting good food at bargain prices, are often disappointed.

It may be heresy to say this, but it is possible to eat very badly in Paris if you don't know what you're doing. Among the large number of restaurants to choose from, there is only a small percentage – maybe ten per cent – where standards of cuisine, service, ambience and value for money are high. And if you come to Paris for only a few days, a week or two weeks a year, you don't want to waste an evening, or several evenings, on

mediocre food when you could be eating really well a few doors
down the street.

This book is designed to help you avoid the mediocre, to
point you towards 100 budget and mid-price eating-places, plus
another 100 places to drink and buy food, where at worst you'll
eat satisfactorily and at best gloriously (depending on price).
All have been personally tested by us, our main criterion being
whether or not we'd return to a place to eat there again. In
addition we offer a collection of tips, insights and advice about
the rich culture of food in this city, garnered from friends and
contacts and from our own experience over several years.

For us the enjoyment of food is an integral part of travelling,
whether to Paris or anywhere else. A good meal in a pleasant
setting with lively, intelligent company is the high-spot of our
evenings at home and abroad, and not simply a costly or
time-consuming diversion. Most of the restaurants and meals
mentioned in this book – particularly in the Moderate and
Deluxe categories – are for enjoying at some length and leisure.

Equally, though, we realize that most people visiting Paris
will be on moderate incomes and won't be able to eat at the
crème de la crème of Parisian restaurants (a meal at La Tour
d'Argent, Le Grand Véfour or Taillevent can easily cost
500–600 francs). We believe it is possible to eat extremely well.
if not with as much style or sophistication, for far less. Our
choices will enable most people to eat three courses, with wine
and service, for a maximum of 160 francs (about £16 at the time
of writing), down to as little as 50 francs in our Budget category
(our categories and price ranges are explained on p. 28).

Our preferences

But before going on we feel we should declare some prejudices
and personal tastes which have helped shape our choices and
judgements. The first thing we should stress is that although
neither of us is vegetarian, we are both fairly antipathetic to red
meat, particularly beef and steak. Readers will therefore find a
strong emphasis on fish, poultry and rabbit in our menu
choices. While this is certainly not representative of indigenous
French tastes, it reflects a trend in eating habits in Britain
where, according to recent food surveys, the consumption of
red meat is on the wane.

Secondly, there are some popular classic French dishes
which we are opposed to on humanitarian grounds, due to their
method of manufacture. In particular we refer to frogs' legs and

pâté de foie gras. Frogs' legs are now largely imported frozen into France from India and the Far East, where frogs have their legs sliced off with a sharp blade while still alive; legless, they are then left to die slowly in their thousands. *Pâté de foie gras* is produced by force-feeding ducks and geese with corn until their livers (*foies*) are distended to gross proportions.

Obviously some vegetarians would argue with us about the morality of eating any meat at all, since most meat products involve animals in varying degrees of suffering, restriction of freedom or unnatural treatment. We do not claim consistency. Paradoxically, despite the undeniable barbarities mentioned, French husbandry is probably less pernicious than that practised in Britain, though the reasons have nothing to do with a greater respect for animal welfare. Firstly, the enormous area of land available to French agriculture means that intensive methods of rearing animals are not widespread. And secondly, French cooks, both domestic and commercial, have a greater concern for the quality of their produce. Tasteless, factory-farmed British chickens, for example, would probably be unacceptable in France where the vast bulk of poultry is reared free-range. Theirs may be slightly more expensive as a result, but it is firm, fleshy and tasty.

Lastly, we are averse to eating in crowded, 'popular', noisy conditions, or in places designated as trendy or '*branché*', as the French say. Our reasons are both aesthetic and economic, and in general we simply prefer to eat discreetly and quietly in more relaxed, traditional surroundings. So if you have a gregarious desire to be '*à la mode*', most of our restaurant choices won't appeal.

THE RESTAURANTS

We would advise most strongly against eating or drinking on the main fashionable boulevards or opposite well-known tourist sites. Such places, by their very location, serve a mainly itinerant tourist clientele – foreign visitors with too much money and too little discrimination who are likely to visit only once. The best eating-places are those used regularly by French diners and which depend on a steady and returning clientele.

Distances

All the eating-places in this book are in the twenty *arrondissements* of the city of Paris proper, within the old city walls, now marked roughly by the Boulevard Périphérique, the modern ring-road. Compared to a city like London, New York or Chicago, this area is comparatively small – some six miles from north to south and seven miles east to west – and is served by a fast, cheap underground railway system (the Métro). So you should not be afraid to travel to eat – virtually any Métro station can be reached from any other in forty minutes maximum, and most places within the inner *arrondissements* (1er–7e) are within thirty minutes walking time from each other. So be adventurous, break out of your local area, head across town and try somewhere different – you may even discover a new part of Paris in the process.

Weekends and August

Many smaller French restaurants close on Sunday, and some stay closed for Monday too (fish restaurants are nearly always closed on Monday because of the lack of fresh fish). One reason for this is that French employment law requires restaurant workers to have two clear days holiday each week, and many restaurateurs can't afford to bring in additional staff to cover those days. So if you're thinking of missing a meal, Sunday is a good day to choose, although we include a separate index of places that do open on Sunday at the back of the book.

August is more of a problem. Paris virtually closes down for four weeks in the summer as the capital's workers head south *en masse* for the sea and sun. That period used to be the whole of August, but in recent years restaurants have begun to stagger their holidays across July and August. The result is that it is now impossible to predict exactly when or for how long a particular restaurant, bar or food-shop will close in the summer (some close for up to six or eight weeks). In general it's the smaller, family-run places that break for four weeks or more; better bets in August are the larger restaurants in the central area, particularly the big *brasseries* which never close, as well as those serving ethnic food.

Our best advice would be to avoid Paris altogether in August if you want to eat seriously – not only are many places closed, but the weather is usually hot and unsettled and the streets are milling with tourists. And if you must come then, be sure to ring in advance any restaurant you intend visiting.

Eating times

The French tend to eat later than the British or Americans – in the evening they rarely sit down before 20.30, and often don't begin to eat until 21.30 or even 22.00. However, as most restaurants open around 19.30 or 20.00 in the evening, this can be to our advantage. If you want to beat the crush, and get a seat at an otherwise popular eating-place, get in early if you haven't already reserved a table. Similarly at lunchtime – if you arrive between 12.00 and 12.30 you are unlikely to have much problem getting seated and served before the mass of Parisians arrive around 12.45–13.15. Most places take their last lunchtime order around 14.00 and will close for the afternoon around 15.00. In general *brasseries* serve food continuously throughout the day and keep much longer hours than restaurants.

Closing times are variable at many restaurants, particularly in the summer and at weekends, and we have sometimes found it impossible to give specific closing times in the restaurant listings. Those that we do give should be regarded as a guide and not a rule.

Reservations

Many of the restaurants we recommend can get very busy at peak times, particularly those in our Deluxe category. For eating out in the evenings between Thursday and Sunday we would advise making a reservation by phone, or better still, calling personally, if you don't want to be disappointed. Generally speaking it's not necessary to reserve a table at lunchtimes.

Improvising

OK, you're stuck in an unfamiliar part of the city and none of our choices are close by or open that night – so how do you choose a good place to eat? These are the clues you should look out for:

* Absence of English or other foreign-language promotion or menu-translations. Restaurants appealing to passing foreigners are generally a poor bet.
* Recent reviews or French guide-book recommendations in

the window. These are often a good sign of above-average standards. In particular, look out for a recent Gault-Millau or Bottin-Gourmand recommendation. These are two of the most reliable and prestigious accolades in French restaurant criticism, and don't necessarily imply high prices either.

* Is the place busy, and are the customers mainly French rather than tourists? It's only common sense to avoid empty restaurants and tourist haunts.
* Does the place look well established, or does it look like a new arrival in the area? Plump for the well-established place every time, because it has probably established some local reputation and a regular clientele.
* Does the restaurant claim a speciality, either a regional cuisine or a particular type of dish? 'Generalist' restaurants, offering a wide range of dishes and styles, are more likely to do everything indifferently.
* Does the restaurant do a reasonably-priced fixed menu, with a good range of choices? If so, and even if you do choose wrongly, you won't spend a lot of money in the process.

THE MENU

The fixed menu

One of the laudable conventions that can make Paris a cheap place to eat is the fixed menu, or '*le menu*', as opposed to '*la carte*' which is the full list of dishes. Other names for it are '*le menu conseillé*', '*le menu promotionnel*' or '*prix fixe*', though if you see it described as '*le menu touristique*', don't bother – that usually means food of an 'international' flavour that they can foist off on unsuspecting visitors. *Le menu* is an all-in price, usually for three courses from a restricted list of items (including the dish of the day), and is always considerably cheaper than the same items ordered à la carte. Sometimes wine is included in the price (*boisson comprise* or '*b.c.*'), sometimes not; service is generally included, but there are exceptions.

In most cases we recommend *le menu* as offering the best value, and in several cases we actively urge against eating à la carte. One of the effects of the recent French tax on 'entertainment' has been to force even some of the more expensive restaurants to offer fixed menus, particularly at lunchtime, thus enabling the less affluent amongst us to sample a little bit of luxury at reduced prices. In fact certain restaurants are included here on the basis of their fixed menu only – eating à la carte would take you over our price-limit of 160 francs.

However, there are certain things to look out for. Many restaurants operate *le menu* only at lunchtime, or until a certain time in the evening (21.00 for example). Alternatively, the price of the set menu may be raised by 15 or 20 francs in the evening. This can of course work to the advantage of those willing to eat their main meal at midday. But when checking places out during the day, beware of such practices.

Similarly some restaurants, while offering a cheap set menu without drink, compensate by selling more expensive wines. You may find, for example, that they don't stock a house wine or *vin ordinaire*. Some also have the irritating habit of offering what seems to be a cheap set menu and then adding '*suppléments*' of a few francs to many of the dishes, which can rapidly hike up the bill. These places are best avoided, though we have included a few which nevertheless offer outstanding value.

The 'plat du jour'

Most restaurants, in addition to their standard menu, offer one or more special '*plats du jour*' which change daily. These are invariably good value, as the ingredients will have been freshly bought that day, and because they're always popular there's likely to be a rapid turnover which ensures that each dish is freshly cooked.

Lunch v. dinner

Many of the places we recommend suggest themselves either as ideal for lunch or more appropriate for eating out in the evening. (Some of course only open for one or the other.) A few restaurants which are suitable for both meals are liable to change their character considerably from midday to evening: at lunch they might be packed with a heterogeneous mix of workers eating quickly and casually, and in the evening have a more sophisticated ambience, with more middle-class couples and families taking a relaxed and leisurely dinner. We have tended to recommend the cheaper places in our Budget bracket as suitable lunchtime venues, and if you are strapped for cash it certainly pays to eat your main meal at midday.

Vegetarians in Paris

Paris is not an easy city for vegetarians. French cuisine relies heavily on animal protein – beef, pork, duck and lamb in large quantities are seen as essential to good eating. First courses are generally not a problem – most restaurants offer excellent salads or *crudités* – but despite the wide range of excellent vegetables in the shops and markets, their presence in main courses tends to be very sparing.

Although there are some vegetarian restaurants in Paris, they are not very popular or well promoted. We have managed to review seven which are partly or wholly vegetarian, or where non-meat-eaters should be able to dine satisfactorily, and since they are so scarce, we list a further seven below that we were unable to visit. We can't vouch for their prices or quality, but we would welcome comments and reviews from vegetarian readers for future reference.

The one regional cuisine which concentrates heavily if not exclusively on vegetables is from Nice in the south of France – any restaurant with the word '*Niçoise*' in its title or description is therefore a good vegetarian bet. Remember too that a *couscous*, with its large bowl of vegetable broth, can be satisfactorily shared between a vegetarian and non-vegetarian.

Additional vegetarian restaurants:

L'Arbre à Souhait, 15 Rue du Jour, 1er (M^o *Les Halles*)
  Tel: 42.33.27.69
Auberge 'In', 34 Rue du Cardinal Lemoine, 5e (M^o *Cardinal Lemoine*) *Tel*: 43.26.43.51
Le Bol en Bois, 35 Rue Pascal, 13e (M^o *Les Gobelins*)
  Tel: 47.07.27.24
Au Grain de Folie, 24 Rue de la Vieuville, 18e (M^o *Abbesses*)
  Tel: 42.58.15.57
Le Jardin, 100 Rue du Bac, 7e (M^o *Rue du Bac* or *Sèvres-Babylone*) *Tel*: 42.22.81.56
La Microbiotèque, 17 Rue de Savoie, 6e (M^o *Saint-Michel*)
  Tel: 43.25.04.96
Naturalia, 107 Rue Caulaincourt, 18e (M^o *Lamarck-Caulaincourt*) *Tel*: 42.62.33.68

THE FOOD
Seasons

Paris can get very hot during the summer months and the heat can dramatically affect your appetite for some French culinary

classics. *Cassoulet*, *pot-au-feu* and other heavy meat dishes are
best avoided in such weather. We've tried to indicate which
restaurants we think should be visited during the cooler
months, and which are more suitable for hot, summer
evenings.

Bloody meat

The French almost always serve beef, steak and lamb (and
sometimes even duck) '*saignant*' – very lightly cooked and
oozing with blood. This is usually much too rare for most
English palates. On ordering, always specify '*à point*' if you
want it cooked medium-rare, and '*bien cuit*' if you want it well
cooked, though the waiter will no doubt wince at such
Anglo-Saxon barbarity!

One of the more pleasing features of French taste in meat is
the fascinatingly wide range of parts of an animal that they are
prepared to cook and consume. Unlike in Britain, there is no
hierarchy of cuts or types of meat, and no negative associations
attach to offal. In France they make a delicacy of *rognons*
(kidneys), tripe (as in *tripes au Calvados*), *pied de porc* (pig's
trotter, as served with *choucroute*) and *cervelles de veau*
(veal-brain), and prices are generally not much different from
other main dishes. So throw off your prejudices and try some of
these esoteric cuts and organs. They really are an eye-opener.

Nouvelle cuisine

Nouvelle cuisine, probably the most controversial
development in French cooking this century, deserves some
explanation. The term was invented in the early 1970s by the
influential food critics Henry Gault and Christian Millau to
describe a style of cooking which was a reaction to the richness
and heaviness of French classical bourgeois cuisine. Its major
emphasises are on a lighter style of cooking (particularly of
sauces), a greater use of vegetables (often puréed), unusual
combinations of ingredients (fruit and meat is quite common)
and stylish presentation, with lots of colour contrast. Many
critics think that this aesthetic approach to food preparation
has been achieved at the expense of taste; others that it is
simply a way of serving less food for more money – a criticism
clearly taken on board, since in recent years there has been a
swing towards larger portions.

These days few restaurants practise *nouvelle cuisine* with the same dedication as in the 1970s (**Chez Pento**, 5N, is the only one included in this book). But what is interesting is the way that the *nouvelle* influence has filtered into the mainstream cuisine – usually, in our opinion, for the better, with new, interesting and often bold combinations of ingredients and flavours which wouldn't have been attempted twenty years ago. Some of the *nouvelle*-inspired dishes sampled for this book turned out to be the most memorable, and not simply because of their appearance. And in the summer months particularly, the lighter style of cuisine, often with an accent on fish, seafood or poultry, can be very welcome.

The cholesterol/calorie factor

French cuisine has a reputation for being full of things which taste good but do your heart, bowels and waistline nothing but harm, and this reputation is deserved. Paris seems to have generated a breed of chefs who can do magical things with all that surplus Euro-fat, with the result that your carefully controlled high-fibre, low-fat diet can disappear as fast as a chocolate mousse the minute you step over a restaurant doorstep.

Of course if you want to stick rigidly with your hyper-healthy eating habits you shouldn't be in Paris at all. Damage limitation is the name of the game, and we have some modest suggestions which will probably keep you alive until you return to the muesli-belt and all that frantic jogging. The best advice we can give has actually nothing to do with eating but with what you might do when you're not. In between gorging yourselves in some of the great restaurants we've found, walk, jog or sprint, but keep moving because that may be the only thing between you and looking like a Michelin tyre ad. (Paris is the best city in the world for those on foot, particularly at night.) Here are some other suggestions:

* Skip breakfast! Continental breakfasts are high in fat, low in fibre, and expensive (unfortunately many hotels now make breakfast compulsory, as part of the all-in price). Buy some fruit instead and eat on the run – you'll save money and calories.
* *Baguettes* are better than *croissants*. The French are wedded to white bread (yes, we think it's delicious too) and eat great quantities of it, though wholemeal bread (*pain complet*) can now be found in many Parisian *boulangeries*. The traditional

baguette, provided it's not smothered in butter, is a relatively healthy choice, but the same cannot be said for those delicious savoury-filled *croissants* made with butter and sugar.

★ Fruit is a good stop-gap for when you get peckish. In hot weather carry a small bottle of mineral water, or search out one of Paris's hundreds of drinking-fountains. Water is healthier than beer or a fizzy drink and will save you a small fortune in café bills.

★ Opt for white meat and fish – both are relatively low in animal fats compared with red meats. Animals which have led active lives usualy have a high ratio of lean meat to fat, so rabbit and game are also a good healthy choice.

★ Don't butter your bread – get the French habit and eat bread *au naturel*, even with cheese.

★ Beware of processed snacks – they are usually unhealthy and expensive.

★ Remember that you are not obliged to eat three courses in even the poshest restaurant – in many of the places we recommend an entrée and main course will be sufficient for the heartiest of appetites.

★ When choosing from the cheese-board, choose the creamier, soft cheeses like Brie and Camembert which, surprisingly, have lower fat contents than the harder cheeses.

★ The French seem to prefer their food salty, so check before adding salt yourself.

Desserts

In some restaurants, à la carte desserts can be expensive (as much as 25–30F) and not very good value. Unless you know a place has a good reputation for its sweets, the final course is the one to miss out if you want to save money. Or you can share one between two of you – it will not be frowned on if you do. If you are dining in the daytime another money-saving suggestion is to pass up the dessert and buy a *pâtisserie* or ice-cream near by to eat out (see the 'Best of the Rest' listings at the end of each section for recommended places to buy these).

WINE
In restaurants

The French have a saying: 'a meal without wine is like a day without sunshine'. Wine enhances the flavour and enjoyment of most French cuisine (though we stop short of the French habit of drinking wine with curries), and in calculating our price-guides we have allowed for half a bottle (sometimes 50cl) of the house wine, or the cheapest bottle available, where wine is not already included in the set menu.

Most wine on French menus is comparatively expensive – the mark-up in restaurants seems to be roughly three times the retail price, compared with twice the retail price in Britain. The result is that wine in restaurants, except for the very cheapest *vin de table* served in a carafe or *pichet* (small jug), is about the same price as in Britain. And also, of course, the more expensive the original bottle, the higher the final price on the menu. So unless you're a dedicated wine connoisseur with money to burn, in most restaurants we would recommend sticking either with the wine served by the carafe or *pichet* or with the bottle described as '*cuvée du patron*' or '*vin de la maison*'. The quality of house wine is generally quite acceptable, no doubt because the reputation of the restaurant is automatically linked to their 'own' wine. In general it seems more difficult to get cheaper white wine than red in many places. Rosé is becoming more and more popular in France, particularly chilled (always!) in summer months, and is a good accompaniment to many of the ethnic cuisines such as *antillais*, North African and *réunionnais*.

If you do choose more expensively, ensure that the bottle is brought to the table before being opened – one trick of the trade is the substituting of a cheaper wine for the one ordered. And the wine should blend with the meal, matching it for quality: if your more expensive wine overwhelms the food then you've either 'over-bought' for the standard of cuisine, or the food wasn't very good in the first place.

A WARNING: the French have several centuries' experience of drinking wine throughout the day (though even they are cutting back on lunchtime drinking these days). The British don't. In many restaurants listed in this book a substantial *pichet* of wine is included in the set menu price, and it can be a very tempting lunchtime treat. But unless you plan to sit or lie around in a park for the afternoon, we would strongly advise moderation, otherwise you can easily wipe out an entire afternoon's sightseeing, particularly in hot summer weather. Have beer or mineral water instead as a less intoxicating alternative.

Wine-bars

The other way of enjoying wine, of course, is in a wine-bar or '*bistro à vin*', either on its own or with a *tartine* (open

sandwich) or cheese and bread. We list several of these in our
'Best of the Rest' listings at the end of each *arrondissement*
section. Opening times of French wine-bars are a little
eccentric – most open early in the morning for the many
near-alcoholic French men and women who want to 'kill the
worm' (*tuer le ver*), as it is known. But, with one or two
exceptions (such as *La Tartine* in the 4ᵉ and *Au Sauvignon* in
the 7ᵉ) they also close early in the evening, around 19.30 or
20.00, so late-night wine-drinking, after a meal, is a little
difficult. And hardly any are open on Sundays.

Wine in wine-bars may be bought by the bottle or the glass.
There is, however, no standard 'glass' in France: the price may
be as low as 3F in some of the cheaper bars, but this is usually for a
7cl or 8cl glass, considerably smaller than our semi-standard
12cl Paris goblet which contains a sixth of a bottle. More
upmarket wine-bars tend to serve wine in larger glasses and the
prices will reflect that. If you're with a group, buying wine by
the bottle is always more economical.

Buying wine to bring home

It's quite a tradition for British tourists to come back from
France loaded up with cheap French wine. At the time of
writing the allowance is about 11 bottles per person, provided it
is bought in France (rather than at duty-free airport or ferry
shops, which have always been a bad deal anyway) and that you
are bringing in no spirits. However, it should be noted that the
differential between French and British wine prices has
steadily been eroded in Britain's favour over the last few years.
Nowadays it is only the very basic *vin de table* and *vin ordinaire*,
in the 6–10F a bottle range, which is substantially cheaper in
France. As a general rule any bottle of wine from a named
region (an *Appellation Controllée* or VDQS wine) at more
than 20F can be bought for roughly the same price in Britain.
And on wine in the 12–15F range the saving is likely to be so
little – about 50–70p on equivalent bottles in British
supermarkets – that it is scarcely worth the trouble to bring it
home.

THE BILL
Service charges

Most French restaurants now add an obligatory service charge
of 15% (more rarely 12%) to the bill, and this will be indicated
on the menu or on your final bill. Often however the words

'*service non compris*' (*s.n.c.*) or '*service en sus*' (service on top) appear on the menu in quite small letters, so make sure you know where you stand. (We specify restaurant policy on this vexed question at the head of each review.) If the menu includes the words '*service compris*' or '*prix net*' it means that the service charge has been incorporated into the price of each dish. In neither case are you obliged or expected to leave an additional gratuity.

Credit cards and cheques

Not many French restaurants accept credit cards or cheques (even Eurocheques backed with a card). This may be a function of distrust (the cheque guarantee system doesn't seem to have spread to France), good economics (avoiding high commissions charged by credit card companies) or possible tax evasion (cheques have to go through the books), but whatever it is, never assume that a card 'will do nicely' because most often it won't. Although the card system is slowly catching on, in general only the larger eating-places with a more affluent, international clientele take plastic. We specify clearly at the head of each entry whether a restaurant takes credit cards – if there's no mention of it, then be prepared to get out your purse or wallet.

Tricks of the trade

There are several ploys to look out for in French restaurants and bars:

* '*Le sous-marin*' (submarine) – an attempted sleight-of-hand practised by some waiters, by which they leave your small change in the saucer *under* the bill and any notes due to you, in the hope that you'll just pick up the notes and forget the coins beneath.
* Many cafés, particularly in tourist areas, increase their prices after 22.00 and hope that customers simply won't notice.
* In cafés, always specify if you want a large or a small beer or *café crème* – if you don't you'll be given a large one, which can prove very expensive.
* If you drink beer at the counter in a bar or café you'll generally be given the cheaper beer on tap – '*à la pression*' – but if you sit at a table then expect to be served a more expensive foreign bottle. Drinking or eating at the bar is always considerably cheaper than sitting down at a table.

26

* If you're eating in a group of two or more, and more than one person orders the same dish, you will usually be served a smaller 'double portion'. For this reason it always pays for everyone to order a different dish.

A GUIDE TO THE GUIDE

The first thing to say in introducing our selection of restaurants is that it is possible to eat in many different contexts – bars, cafés and *salons de thé* all serve food of differing quality and quantity, from the humble sandwich to more ambitious cooked meals. But with the exception of two beloved wine-bars which serve food, we've made our main selection from the ranks of *bona fide* restaurants. These include some that would be more properly described as bistros (small, usually family-run restaurants serving a fairly narrow range of often regional cuisine). Others are fully-fledged, authentic *brasseries* (large, Alsatian in origin, specializing in *choucroute* and seafood, and usually open till the small hours). But all serve conventional, sit-down, three-course meals with table service.

The guide is organized around the *arrondissement* plan of the city of Paris proper which, if you look on a map, spiral out clockwise from the 1er *arrondissement* in the centre. Each of the twelve sections of the book covers one or a pair of *arrondissements*. About two-thirds of our choices are in the inner ten *arrondissements*; the rest are spread out in the outlying *arrondissements* (11e–20e). We have, however, omitted the gastronomically barren 16e *arrondissement* as a separate section: it contains only one restaurant, **La Ficotière**, that we can recommend, and our review can be found in the section covering the 1er and 8e *arrondissements*. The 17e, on the other hand, we do cover even though we recommend no restaurants there at all – just a few excellent food-shops which are listed among the 'Best of the Rest' at the end of its section.

Each section is introduced by a brief description of the area, advising on quirky, lesser-known things to look out for and giving some of its flavour and history. Where possible we try to relate that history and local character to the kind of eating-place and cuisine found there.

We have tried to include a wide spectrum of cuisines and styles of food, from classical bourgeois cooking and a variety of regional cuisines to *nouvelle cuisine* and 'ethnic' food. Like Britain, France, and particularly Paris, has incorporated a wide range of ethnic cuisines. Twenty per cent of our choices are non-French: Algerian, Congolese, *antillais*, Jewish, Indonesian, Vietnamese, Russian and several others. However, as a matter of policy we have avoided cuisines which are widely available in Britain, such as Chinese, Indian, Greek and Italian – we see little point in going to Paris for more of the same. Indian restaurants in particular do not offer the same good value that they do in Britain.

Fish dishes are served in most restaurants in Paris, but few specialize in fish and they tend to be rather expensive. However, we have managed to find about ten places within our price range which serve a variety of fish and seafood. Tuesdays and Fridays are traditionally the best days for eating in fish restaurants, to sample fish at its freshest, and as a rule the large *brasseries*, with their own fresh *coquillage* stalls outside on the pavement, seem to give the best value in seafood (which is curious, since Alsace is a long, long way from the sea).

Indexes

At the back of the book we have provided separate indexes with map references: (i) all the restaurants covered, listed alphabetically; (ii) restaurants specializing in fish; (iii) restaurants serving vegetarian dishes; (iv) restaurants serving non-French cuisine; (v) late-closing restaurants; and (vi) restaurants open on Sundays. In addition there is an index of wine-bars, food-shops, etc. ('Best of the Rest'), and a brief index of French culinary terms.

Price categories

Restaurants are divided by price into three categories within each *arrondissement* section – *Budget*, *Moderate* and *Deluxe*. For a three-course meal, inclusive of wine and service, you can expect to pay the following:

Budget – less than 60F

Moderate – 60–120F

Deluxe – 120–160F

These prices are calculated either (a) on the basis of the set menu plus half a bottle or *pichet* of house wine and/or service (where not included), or (b) where there is no set menu, by adding together the average price of three courses à la carte, plus half a bottle of the cheapest wine, plus service. In each entry we also list the price of wine separately so that non-drinkers can calculate the price of a meal without it. Where a set menu price is listed it is always without wine or service unless otherwise indicated. Where a restaurant could fall into more than one category, depending on whether you eat from the set menu or à la carte, we usually categorize it according to the cheaper option.

'The Best of the Rest'

At the end of each area section we list a selection of other food and drink outlets – wine-bars, cafés, food-shops, *salons de thé*, etc. – with brief comments. These are selected for people who want to eat and drink out, rather than those who may want to do their own cooking, so we include *pâtisseries*, *boulangeries* and cheese-shops (good for picnics) but not fresh food shops, markets or butchers.

Finding your way

Each of the restaurants in the main selection is accompanied by a map reference to help you find it using the maps at the front of the book. The number in each reference indicates the *arrondissement* it is in, the letter to its location in that *arrondissement*. With each restaurant address is also given the name of the nearest Métro (M°) station(s). For more precise directions you should refer to one of the several Paris street plans which you can buy in newsagents. We have followed the French convention in abbreviating *arrondissements*: '1er' stands for the *premier arrondissement*, '2e' for the *deuxième*, and so on.

A qualification

While we have taken every precaution to ensure the accuracy of the information in this book, there are bound to be errors. Moreover, the catering trade is a notoriously fickle, fast-turnover industry, and it is estimated that each year some ten per cent of restaurants either close or change hands. Bearing in mind that many of our choices are more stable, long-standing institutions, it is still possible that some of them may have vanished or changed dramatically in the time between our visiting them and your reading this book.

Secondly, the prices quoted in the guide were correct in August 1986. Taking inflation and rising property prices into account, we would expect an annual increase of about five per cent.

One of the best ways in which we can rectify any inaccuracies in future editions is through the vigilant efforts of our readers. Therefore please send us your comments, suggestions, criticisms and corrections at the address given below.

In the meantime – *bon appetit!*

Carl Gardner and Julie Sheppard
c/o Fontana Paperbacks
8 Grafton Street
London W1X 3LA

1er and 8e Arrondissements

Les Halles – Louvre – Palais-Royal – Concorde –
Champs-Élysées – L'Étoile

The strip of central Paris made up of the 1er and 8^e
arrondissements contains a large proportion of the most
historic buildings in the city, and it is difficult to give a fresh
perspective on it in only a few hundred words. This is the core
of tourist Paris, immortalized in a mountain of guide-books,
yet even here there are controversial transformations afoot.

At the heart of the area is the Louvre–Tuileries–Champs-
Élysées axis, climbing to the Arc de Triomphe at L'Étoile – an
extraordinary urban space over two miles long which set the
pattern for so much of the development of the city. Of the
Louvre enough has been written, except that soon there'll be
even more miles of corridor and gallery to tramp when the
Ministry of Finance moves out of the wing by the Rue de

Rivoli, giving the whole edifice over to Art with a capital A. By then, too, Mr Pei will have built his mysterious glass pyramid just east of the Place du Carrousel, on top of the new complex of passageways and underground galleries. And that will be the biggest change here since the burning down of the Tuileries Palace in 1871.

Passing through the Jardin des Tuileries (by night Paris's main gay cruising spot), we come to the Place de la Concorde, designed by the architect Jacques-Ange Gabriel in 1753 in honour of Louis XV whose son, ironically, was to be guillotined here less than forty years later. Then up the Champs-Élysées, now largely spoiled as a promenade by the growing intrusion of pavement cafés and the amount of space given over to the motor-car. Anyone who eats or drinks on the Champs-Élysées itself these days has certainly more money than taste.

Of the 8e itself there's little to say except that it's expensive and barren, particularly after dark when the chic boutiques and *haute couture* houses close down. On the northern edge there's the pretty, fashionable Parc de Monceau, and south of the Champs-Élysées are the two magnificent exhibition halls, the Grand and Petit Palais. The former mounts some of the city's most prestigious art-shows, and it's almost worth the entry fee just to walk inside the enormous span of glass and iron with its unexpected *fin-de-siècle* ornamentation. The back part of the building houses Paris's equivalent of South Ken's Science Museum, the Palais de la Découverte, a great treat for young and old alike.

But enough of the 8e. Let's flip back to the 1er for something far less precious, the grossly glorified shopping-mall of Les Halles. Built on the site of the old market, which was demolished in 1969 after years of campaigns to save it, the complex is still incomplete though the wonderful children's playground is now functioning (pity they don't let us adults in!). Despite – or because of – its hi-tech flashiness, the whole Les Halles area with its surrounding streets – Pierre-Lescot, Rambuteau and Saint-Denis – is now a serious right-bank rival to the Latin Quarter for night-life. And there are a surprising number of good eating-places to be found, some of them undoubtedly remnants of the old Les Halles, now gone up-market.

If you want further evidence that even this historic heart of Paris is on the move, visit the Palais-Royal where you'll stumble across one of Mitterand's boldest – or maddest – public art commissions, Daniel Buren's *Les Deux Plateaux*, a geometric series of striped, broken columns arranged where Cardinal Richelieu once used to stroll.

Note: for convenience we have included in this section the one solitary restaurant we can recommend in the barren 16e *arrondissement* – **La Ficotière**, just outside the border of the 8e, close to L'Étoile.

BUDGET

La Fauvette   **Map Ref: 1A**
6 Rue Saint-Honoré (M° *Louvre*)
Tel: 42.36.75.85
Open: lunch only
Closed: Saturday, Sunday
Set menu: 37F
Wine: 22–32F (litre)
Service: 12%

A great little lunchtime place, between Les Halles and the Louvre, where the visitor can benefit from cheap eating for the local workers. Apart from its excellent 37F menu (service and wine not included), it's notable for its helpful, friendly staff – quite rare in a place like this where the pace can get frenetic and tempers frayed, especially in hot weather.

Although you can eat à la carte, it's really not worth straying from the set menu which includes most of what's good on their short, businesslike menu. Starters include the usual range: a very good rabbit pâté; carrot and tomato salad; sardines and *saucisson*. For the main dish *lapin chasseur*, with boiled potatoes, is a great success – tender, gamy rabbit in a rich white wine, onion and tomato sauce. Other strong contenders are the garlicky *pintadeau froid* (baby guinea-fowl with salad; *bavette échalote* (steak and shallots); and *épaule d'agneau*. Even the desserts won't let you down: the *clafouti* and the *gâteau de riz* (rice, caramel and raisins) were voted 'the best 37F desserts in Paris' by one group of discerning diners. But stay off the chocolate mousse – not the finest of its kind, by any means.

With a 25cl *pichet* of wine each (it's lunchtime, remember!) plus coffee, you'll come out well under 60F, and so substantially fed you may even want to skip dinner.

La Fresque   Map Ref: 1B

100 Rue Rambuteau (M° *Étienne-Marcel* or *Les Halles*)
Tel: 42.33.17.56
Open: lunch and dinner until midnight
Closed: Sunday lunch
Set menu: 43F, two courses including wine, coffee and service
À la carte: 90–110F, service at 15%
Wine: 28–32F (litre)

Hard by the north side of the Les Halles glitterama boutique
complex, this laid-back joint, run by a youthful staff, is an
excellent cheap place for either lunch or dinner. Especially
interesting too for vegetarians or semi-vegetarians, and for
hot, summer eating, as the menu is very light on meat, strong
on fish, eggs and vegetables, and always includes one
vegetarian dish each day.

At lunchtime there's a two-course 43F set menu, including
drink, coffee and service. On our visit, Baltic herring, *salade
amande* or *fromage blanc* with sorrel to start; *cereals légumes*
(brown rice with a vegetable ragout), *filet de rascasse meunière*
(hogfish) or *côte de porc moutarde ancienne* (pork chop in a
mustard sauce, again served with rice) to follow. À la carte,
there's a nicely cosmopolitan range of starters – tarama,
taboulleh, Greek salad, *moules tahitiennes* and *chèvre chaud
sur toast* (toasted goat's cheese) – to set up the palate for a
choice of poached haddock, *hamburger œuf à cheval*, *bavette
aux échalotes* or *œufs brouillés aux fines herbes*. In the evening
there's a slightly broader menu, incorporating favourites like
trout and rabbit. For three courses, in a pleasantly relaxed
setting (it used to be a snail shop), you could get away with little
more than 100F.

L'Incroyable   Map Ref: 1C

26 Rue de Richelieu (M° *Palais-Royal*)
Tel: 42.96.24.64
Open: lunch and dinner until 20.30
Closed: Saturday dinner, Sunday, Monday dinner
Set menu: 38F, wine and service included

Like several of the cheapest restaurants in Paris, L'Incroyable
consists of two crowded rooms, which are little more than
converted parlours, on either side of a covered alleyway. These

are packed at all hours and you're as likely to be squeezed up against office workers from the nearby banking centres as manual workers who've strayed over from the never-ending dig at Les Halles. The set menu is short, predictable, but sound. Among the starters it is interesting to see *salade mexicaine* (rice, sweetcorn, peppers, etc.) creeping in alongside traditional pâté and *œuf mayonnaise*. Main courses are steak, veal, roast pork and *tripes à la Caen*, all served with delicious crispy *pommes frites*. (For 12F extra you can have the *confit de canard* – two succulent duck drumsticks.) Rounded off with the ubiquitous chocolate mousse, almost the only dessert which isn't an extra 5F, and including mineral water or wine, for a basic price of 38F this place is certainly a little unbelievable. And to walk off your ample lunch you can go just down the street to the elegant Palais-Royal gardens.

Luinaud   **Map Ref: 8A**
Cité Berryer, 24 Rue Boissy-d'Anglas (M° *Madeleine*)
Tel: 42.65.64.90
Open: lunch and dinner until 22.00
Closed: Saturday dinner, Sunday
À la carte: 50–60F
Wine: 4F (20cl)
Service: 10%

Close by Concorde and the Madeleine, just off the Rue Saint-Honoré, the most amazing thing about Luinaud is that it still exists at all in this very chic area. But exist it does, and a welcome haven of cheap, honest eating in the land of the 400F lunch. But as a result it gets crowded for lunch during the week. Run by a friendly old couple, Luinaud displays all those features of the traditional family-run concern: unchanging brown and white décor, large mirrors, and a hand-written, mimeographed menu. And as often in such establishments, menu choices are simple but sound: pâté, egg mayonnaise, tuna, mackerel, garlic sausage or sardines (served in their tin!) for starters. Main courses are very meat-based: pork, beef tongue, sirloin steak, etc. For a hot day they also offer *viandes froides*, generous slices of cold pork and roast beef (not too bloody), served with excellent hot sauté potatoes and a small green salad. Very substantial. Desserts too are rather predictable – stewed fruit, mousse, pineapple – but the individual fruit tarts looked the best bet. This whole mini-feast, ideal for a sight-seeing lunch, will set you back just over 50F. If you skip the wine or miss the dessert you could even dip under that. And as you waddle back down to Concorde you can look in the windows of Maxims and congratulate yourself on your economy.

Le Relais du Sud-Ouest   **Map Ref: 1D**
154 Rue Saint-Honoré (Mᵒ *Palais-Royal* or *Louvre*)
Tel: 42.60.62.01
Open: lunch and dinner until 22.30
Closed: Sunday
Set menus: 48F, 120F, wine and service included

You will have gathered that French food is very meat-based, and unless you go to specialist restaurants, of which there are few, it's very difficult to eat meatlessly. Today, for lunch, we managed it, and very good it was too. This lovely little bistro-bar is just a spit from the Louvre, yet curiously it hasn't been discovered by screaming hordes of tourists who for some reason prefer to eat at the over-priced plastic palaces on the Rue de Rivoli.

As its name suggests, the owners of this place come from south-west France, and the small dining areas in front of and behind the bar are decorated with regional memorabilia. The food also reflects their origins, with cider on offer as well as beer and wine, and several of the dishes on the excellent 48F menu show a distinct regional flair. *Hors d'œuvres* include a rich *terrine de campagne*, a celery salad and a crispy lettuce salad dressed in walnut oil. Main courses include veal sweetbreads with creamed rice, *andouillette bordelaise* (Bordeaux sausage) with *pommes frites*, lamb with flageolet beans and *brochette de dinde* (turkey kebab) with a *gratin* of courgettes. Not, you will agree, your average café fare, and the really great thing about this place is that it usually serves a vegetarian dish; on the day we visited, a superb *gratin d'aubergines*. Wonderful!

Finish off with a slice of apple or strawberry tart or cheese, and throw in a glass of beer (*compris*), and you'll find your money's been well spent. But get in soon after midday if you don't want to be crowded out by the discerning French who flock here in droves.

Le Stado

Map Ref: 1E

150 Rue Saint-Honoré (M° *Louvre* or *Palais-Royal*)
Tel: 42.60.29.75
Open: lunch and dinner until 23.00 every day
Closed: Sunday
Set menus: 48F (lunch), 65F (dinner), wine and service
included
À la carte: not recommended

Another lovely little lunch-place close by the Louvre which the tourists don't seem to have discovered. And like its near neighbour, the **Relais du Sud-Ouest** (1D), it specializes in the cuisine of the French Pyrenees. Owned by a French rugby star, its décor is a curious combination of rugby photos and fake barn-like accoutrements, including hanging mangers of hay and several stuffed animals staring down at you. You can eat à la carte, and there's an expensive 120F menu with *confit de canard*, but we wouldn't recommend either – stick with the 48F menu (rising to 65F in the evening) and you'll be well pleased.

Starters are humdrum but substantial – *fromage de tête vinaigrette* (rather like a cross between brawn and corned beef), *crudités*, pâté, etc – while main dishes, which change daily, are in the south-western meaty tradition. For example, there's *épaule d'agneau rôti* with *ratatouille*, *foie aux oignons* (liver and onions) and *pommes frites*, *boudin basque* or *pavé rumpsteak*. Rabbit and poultry figure too: a *poulet basquaise* and a hearty *lapin chasseur* with small pasta *coquillettes* complete the list.

The *tarte aux pommes* and *tarte aux abricots* of the house are particularly luscious examples of the species, and besides the pastries there's also *fromage blanc* and *moka glacé*. And after that little lot you'll be well set up to tackle the second half of your expedition round the Louvre. Or perhaps not.

MODERATE

L'Épi d'Or   **Map Ref: 1F**
25 Rue Jean-Jacques Rousseau (M° *Louvre* or *Palais-Royal*)
Tel: 42.36.38.12
Open: lunch and dinner until 22.30
Closed: Sunday
Set menu: 90F, wine included
À la carte: 140–150F
Wine: 38F (bottle)
Service: 15%
Credit cards: Visa

Sometimes one can complain that French portions are a little on the small side for the English stomach. Well it's not a complaint heard here: this is a place where you'll come away groaning, and not at the quality or the prices. The interior is pleasantly cluttered, not to say cramped, with the old-fashioned counter loaded with an assortment of gâteaus, just to give a hint of what's to come.

The menu is broad, embracing traditional favourites like *cassoulet*, *saumon grillé*, *bœuf rôti* and *palette de porc provençale* (blade of pork), as well as several more exotic items such as *cassolette de calmar à l'américaine* (casserole of squid), *osso bucco* and *curry de volailles*. The 90F set menu includes rump steak and *escalope de veau*, but the *rognons d'agneau* (lamb's kidneys) were deliciously tender and barbecued on a skewer with parsley and butter, served with an enormous platter of fresh, crisp *pommes frites*. The very palatable house red (included in the set price) comes in a generous pitcher, and a bottle of chilled mineral water is served as a matter of course to each table.

Having eyed the gâteaus for the best part of an hour whilst we ate the rest of the meal, we couldn't resist any longer. Enormous wedges of lemon tart duly arrived, the best we'd ever had, each topped with whipped cream and dusted with sugar. The chocolate gâteau came with an extra topping of chocolate sauce: *mmm*! From all this we came away happy, replete and only just over 100F a head poorer. Definitely a place for '*la grande bouffe*'.

La Ficotière

Map Ref: 16A

17 Rue Jean-Giraudoux (M° *Kléber*)
Tel: 47.23.66.55
Open: lunch and dinner until 22.00
Closed: Sunday
Set menu: 102F, wine and service included
Credit cards: Visa

In general L'Étoile is a lethal eating-area – prices are astronomical at most places within striking distance of the Champs-Élysées. Here's an exception, just over the border in the 16e, which is a good standby for people up in that area. The formula here is a little puzzling at first, with what looks like a range of set menus from 102F to 250F, but all that distinguishes them is the wine: the food stays the same. For your 250F you get a bottle of champagne, if you're in expansive mood, but for 102F it's merely a very acceptable Cabernet Rouge . . . but as much of it as you can drink! ('*À volonté*' means what it says, so if you're having lunch, go steady, unless you want to be staggering round the Arc de Triomphe the rest of the day.)

The place itself is clean and modern, with the kitchen in full view of the diners, and an extremely friendly patron will patiently explain his novel menu. But it's all quite simple – to start you help yourself at the overwhelming salad/*hors d'œuvres* bar which contains virtually every entrée, vegetable and salad you've ever seen, and some more, in dozens of bowls. And if you don't take enough the patron will gently reprimand you! You could pile up herring, *chorizo* (Spanish sausage), egg, sweetcorn, beetroot, vegetable mayonnaise salad, tomato, cucumber . . .

To follow there is a range of about six main dishes, which change daily, generally served with *pommes frites*. Pick of the day was a *côtelette Pajarski* with *sauce bourguignonne*, which is a perfectly sautéed beef and veal rissole. Then there were *onglets à la sauce moutarde*, *rougets grillés*, *brochettes d'agneau* and *tranchons de canard* – a good, sound but simple range of fish, meat and poultry. Desserts are basic but satisfying: *mousse framboise* (very fruity) or *mousse chocolat*, *crème caramel* or cheese.

A meal at La Ficotière won't be the gastronomic highlight of your holiday, but for a tenner, in this area, it's good value. And salad-lovers and wine-drinkers will be more than pleased.

DELUXE

Chez Denise • **Map Ref: 1G**
5 Rue des Prouvaires (M^o *Louvre*, *Châtelet* or *Les Halles*)
Tel: 42.36.21.82
Open: lunch and dinner till dawn
Closed: Sunday
À la carte: 150–170F
Wine: 70F (litre)
Service: 15%

We heard an interesting theory expounded here: that all the old restaurants around Les Halles were so used to feeding big, hulking market porters who needed 5000 calories a day that, despite the closure of the markets in the late sixties, they couldn't get out of the habit. Certainly it's a thesis that holds up in our experience (see also **L'Épi d'Or'**, 1F) – here the sheer quantity of food is overwhelming. No wonder Chez Denise has the fattest cat in the history of France, seen slumped on a barrel by the front door.

But *largesse* is only one of the many merits of this excellent all-night bistro, much frequented by journalists, writers, media people and the like. There really is a Denise – she presides over the long, bustling interior or sits at the front desk like the madam of a bordello, dealing brusquely with those who haven't made a reservation. (We suffered at her hands the first time we tried to get in on spec.) Inside the atmosphere is lively and animated, with even the waiters joining in the fun when they have time. And if you speak any French at all, conversation with adjoining tables just comes naturally. The décor is shabby-chic – lithographs and cartoons crowd the walls, and brass rails, red leather *banquettes*, red checkered tablecloths and old wooden beams abound. You immediately notice nice touches – butter on all the tables, and delicious brown *pain de campagne* instead of the usual white *baguette*.

The menu is written on a movable blackboard. To start, *salade frisée aux croûtons* (crispy lettuce with crispy croutons), mackerel fillets, herring, a wide range of *charcuterie* and pâté, and, when in season, asparagus vinaigrette. The half dozen snails, served hot with butter and garlic, are a real savoury treat.

Main courses include stuffed tomatoes, a superb *lapin à la moutarde*, *haricot de mouton* (a stew of mutton and white

l'agneau meunière (lamb's brains cooked in
... of beef and lamb, *haddock meunière* and
...orain). The Normandy speciality, *tripes au*
... was an eye-opener. If you come from the north of
...gland, forget the sickly white stuff emanating from the old
UCP shops – this tripe is something else: arriving in an
enormous tureen (too much for one person) it takes the form of
a rich, meaty stew with a uniquely delicate flavour and texture.
To help it down the house wine we had was a fruity, slightly
chilled Brouilly (a named Beaujolais).

Desserts are less varied, but favourites seemed to be an
amazing *gâteau Marguerite* with raspberry sauce, and
strawberries and cream – about half a pound each, with thick,
unwhipped cream. The price of this gastronomic route march,
with service and all the trimmings: 160F each. But for
atmosphere, quality of cuisine and sheer generosity, this place
gets top marks. Keep up the good work, Denise.

Madinina   **Map Ref: 1H**

17 Rue Saint-Denis (M° *Châlelet*)
Tel: 42.36.02 75
Open: lunch and dinner until midnight
Closed: Tuesday
À la carte: 140–150F
Wine: from 50F (bottle)
Service: 15%

Possibly the greatest revelation of our whole Parisian sojourn
was the superb quality of *antillais* cuisine. This restaurant
comes out of the same West Indian bag as **La Créole** (14B) and
Le Flamboyant (14C), and is possibly even better than those
two, though slightly more expensive. Centrally situated, and
more discreetly decorated than the others, this place is
extremely popular with West Indian customers, which is
always a good sign. At midday there is a 49F '*menu express*',
though this is not the place to take a hurried lunch – the food
deserves better than that.

The excellent range of starters includes three versions of
accras (cod, crab or shrimp), the famous *crabe farci* and a
refreshing *salade antillaise*, incorporating tomatoes, lettuce,
sweetcorn, shredded cucumber and avocado. Then it's on to all
that's best in Martinique and Guadeloupe cooking: a lightly
curried *colombo d'agneau* or *poulet marsala*; *poulpe* (octopus)

in a delicate, spicy sauce; two classic fish dishes, *blaff de poisson* and *court bouillon de poisson*, both in two versions; more simply *poisson* or *poulet grillé au citron vert* (lime). And as always every dish served with a bowl of rice and delicious spiced kidney beans. However the *pièce de résistance*, *cochon de lait farci* (stuffed suckling pig), topped them all – tender pieces of succulent young pig with crackling, accompanied by an extraordinary stuffing of minced pork, green pepper, breadcrumbs and herbs. *Formidable!* Washed down with a robust, slightly chilled Côtes du Rhône, or a fruity, full Beaujolais, this has to be one of the best treats Paris can offer at this price. Unfortunately, they don't serve it every night, so check first.

Something they do serve every night is the unforgettable *pâtisserie maison*, which goes by the expressive title '*tourment d'amour*' – a sponge sandwich with an almond and caramel filling, wrapped in dried coconut, sprinkled with chocolate, soaked in rum or Grand Marnier, and served hot! Oh, the torment was real . . . And if that doesn't grab you, there are fresh fruit *flambés* or the amazing *Mont Pelé*, a half pineapple filled with vanilla and caramel ice-cream and soaked with rum.

THE BEST OF THE REST

Wine-bars – cafés – bars

Aux Bons Crus, 7 Rue des Petits Champs, 1ᵉʳ (Mᵒ *Bourse* or *Pyramides*) – a workers' wine-bar serving sandwiches and light lunches.

Café-Tabac Henry IV, 13 Place du Pont-Neuf, 1ᵉʳ (Mᵒ *Pont-Neuf*) – a well-situated wine-bar serving a great range of wines, especially from the Loire, and sandwiches.

La Cloche des Halles, 28 Rue Coquillière, 1ᵉʳ (Mᵒ *Les Halles*) – a lovely wine-bar typical of the area, named after the bell which used to open and close the old markets.

Le Cochon à l'Oreille, 15 Rue Montmartre, 1ᵉʳ (Mᵒ *Les Halles*) – a beautiful bar with enormous ceramic murals of the old Les Halles. Open from 5.00 in the morning till 16.30.

Aux Deux Saules, 91 Rue Saint-Denis, 1ᵉʳ (Mᵒ *Les Halles*) – a lively café-bar on the main promenading street of Les Halles.

Sit with the youth and marginals, pull up a drink or cheap meal, and watch the street-life.

Ma Bourgogne, 133 Boulevard Haussmann, 8e (M^o *Miromesnil*) – a serious wine-bar strong on the wines of Macon and the Rhône.

Le Rubis, 10 Rue du Marché-Saint-Honoré, 1er (M^o *Pyramides* or *Tuileries*) – a popular and cheapish *bistro à vin* in an expensive area. Great sandwiches made with *pain poîlane*, and a daily hot dish.

Salons de thé

Fanny Tea, 20 Place Dauphine, 1er (M^o *Pont-Neuf*) – an exquisite old tea-room in this beautiful square tucked away near the Pont-Neuf.

Verlet, 256 Rue Saint-Honoré, 1er (M^o *Palais-Royal*) – a shop selling an enormous range of tea and coffee, with a few tables where you can drink and eat a pastry or two.

Food-shops

Androuet, 41 Rue d'Amsterdam, 8e (M^o *Liège*) – the most famous cheese-shop in Paris, where you can also eat complete cheese-based meals.

Fauchon, 26 Place de la Madeleine, 8e (M^o *Madeleine*) – somewhere to look, rather than buy. We include Paris's best-known food-shop as an example of the extravagant lunacy which bourgeois Paris can conjure up. A quite amazing display of every exotic fruit, vegetable and over-the-top food item you can imagine (over 20,000 in all), which makes Fortnum & Mason look like a village grocers. And if you're after a good bottle of plonk, how about a 1919 Château d'Yquem Sauternes at 5,400F? When an envicus arsonist set fire to the place in 1977, it is said that the flames were fuelled by gallons of extremely expensive cognac in the cellars.

Ferme Saint-Hubert, 21 Rue Vignon, 8e (M^o *Madeleine*) – again a superb cheese-shop (the best Roquefort in town?), with *menu de dégustation*.

La Maison du Chocolat, 225 Rue Faubourg-Saint-Honoré, 8e (M^o *Ternes*) – amongst other brown, sticky delights, it sells the wonderful dark Valrhona chocolate by the bar.

Réné Saint-Ouen, 111 Boulevard Haussmann, 8^e
(M^o *Miromesnil*) – a *boulangerie* selling bread made in the most
fantastic shapes, such as animals, bicycles, horses and carts.

Tachon, 38 Rue de Richelieu, 1er (M^o *Palais-Royal*) – an
old-fashioned neighbourhood *fromagerie* near the Louvre.

2ᵉ Arrondissement

Bourse – Saint-Denis

The smallest *arrondissement* in Paris, enclosed within the
Boulevard de Sebastopol, the '*grands boulevards*' and the Rue
Étienne-Marcel, the 2ᵉ is a commercial area occupied
principally by the garment trade. One of its most interesting
features is its '*passages*' – tall, glass-covered pedestrian arcades
of shops or workshops. In 1840 there were more than 130 of
these, but many were destroyed or fell into disuse with the
coming of the motor-car. One you won't be able to miss, if you
follow our recommendations, is the Passage du Grand-Cerf,
which runs off the Rue Dussoubs beside the **Dona Flor**
restaurant (2D) and the *Fitzcarraldo* bar. But there are several
clusters of these fascinating, romantic covered walkways in the
2ᵉ – for example, at the top end of the Rue Montmartre, off the
Rue Saint-Marc (almost opposite the **Brissemoret**, 2B). Then
there's a complicated pattern of passages north of the Rue de
Caire, off the Rue Saint-Denis, which we recommended
exploring in the daytime only – some of these covered streets

can be very dark and sinister, and some are locked up at night. Possibly the most stylish are the Galleries Colbert and Vivienne, right next to the Bibliothèque Nationale, off the Rue des Petits-Champs; and the most charmingly unspoilt is just over the border in the 1er, the Galerie Véro-Dodat (2 Rue du Bouloi), with its archaic little boutiques – a doll-repairer, a hand-printer and a lute-maker amongst them.

The other major feature of note – if only so that you can avoid it – is the Rue Saint-Denis, the city's main red-light district where an estimated 80% of the city's prostitution takes place. It was here that Shirley Maclaine, method actor to the last, undertook all her research for *Irma la Douce* (filmed in an accurate Hollywood set, incidentally). On the border of the 2^e, where the red-light district suddenly ends as if by magic, stands the imposing Porte Saint-Denis. Dating back to 1672, and replacing the old city gates, it was designed by François Blondel as a triumphal arch to celebrate Louis XIV's victories on the Rhine and in Flanders.

The restaurants in the 2^e, in keeping with the tone of the area, tend to be very much on the traditional side (with the exception of **Dona Flor**'s gay Latin-American flourish), and most of the decent places shut early. **Le Druout** (2A) and **Brissemoret** (2B) sum up the area perfectly – popular but fading remnants of the old heart of the city which is now being invaded and gradually transformed by the social and architectural cataclysms of Les Halles.

BUDGET

Le Druout   **Map Ref: 2A**

103 Rue de Richelieu (M^o *Richelieu-Druout*)
Tel: 42.96.68.23
Open: lunch and dinner until 21.30 every day
À la carte: 40–60F
Wine: 17F (bottle)
Service: 12%

Le Druout, **Chartier** (9A) and **Le Commerce** (15A), all under the same management and with virtually the same menu and prices, offer probably the best food, in the most interesting, authentic surroundings, and for the least money, in the whole of Paris. As such they're an invaluable standby for any visitor to the city, not to mention a large section of its working population. Little changed since the nineteenth century, their décor consists of brass rails, large mirrors and hanging globe lamps. Chartier, with its double height, wood panelled walls and upper gallery, is probably the most impressive though also the most crowded and hectic, while Le Druout has a more elegant charm. In each the service, provided by squads of white-aproned waiters, is unbelievably efficient.

The menu is broad but fairly basic. For *hors d'œuvres*, salads, ham, rabbit pâté, garlic sausage, egg mayonnaise and soup, all between 5F and 10F. Main courses are grilled salmon or *truite meunière* at 26F; a superbly tasty rabbit in tarragon sauce, with sauté potatoes at 28F; lamb chop with *rissolé* potatoes at 23F; and roast chicken and *pommes frites* at 17F.

The wine-list too is a model of economy: the dependable house red is 17F a bottle, a Blanc de Blanc is 18F, and half bottles are always available. In fact no wine here is more than 45F, with the majority at around half that. Desserts are simple, though the ice-creams are pre-packaged and slightly expensive; try instead the chocolate mousse at 6F, fresh pineapple at 10F, or *gâteau Marguerite* (almond cake) at a mere 9F (smothered with Chantilly cream for an extra pittance).

Choose carefully and you can eat three courses here for less than 40F – and you'd be hard pushed to spend more than 70F, with wine. Some people never eat anywhere else.

MODERATE

Brissemoret   Map Ref: 2B

5 Rue Saint-Marc (Mᵒ *Rue Montmartre* or *Bourse*)
Tel: 42.36.91.72
Open: lunch and dinner till 22.30
Closed: Saturday, Sunday
Set menu: 60F (until 20.00)
À la carte: 110–130F
Wine: 50F (bottle)
Service: included

There's a certain tradition in French restaurant décor of deliberate decrepitude, of preservation to the point of virtual collapse. Brissemoret takes this tendency to an extreme, yet manages to serve some of the best food, at the most reasonable prices, in the whole area of the Bourse (stock exchange) – possibly because they've spent nothing on fittings since well before the Wall Street Crash. While all around it becomes more and more chic (witness the trendy eaterie up the street called The Dow Jones), Brissemoret celebrates its authentic status with faded mirrors, worn *banquettes*, rickety chairs, peeling paintwork, tired-looking greenery and some very antique plumbing (such as the radiator near the door which can't be turned off even in summer – hot-weather diners, beware that seat). Yet the half dozen tables are always booked, even at lunchtime, so reservations are imperative.

An excellently balanced menu offers a superb range of entrées: *maquereaux au vin blanc*, for example, is served in a delicate creamy Béarnaise sauce; *champignons à la crème* are fresh, and again lightly sauced; and if those don't appeal there's always *fonds d'artichauts frais* (fresh artichoke hearts), *rillons flambés au Cognac* (crisp belly pork sautéed in Cognac) or *fromage de chèvre chaud* (hot goat's cheese).

Meat and fruit aren't often brought together in French cooking, but here they carry it off to great effect. For example the *côte de porc aux pruneaux* (pork with prunes) or the excellent *pintade aux fruits* – roast guinea-fowl with cooked apricots, carrots and little crisply cooked cabbage, all in a rich lemon (and Marsala?) sauce. *Formidable!* The tender *mignon de porc* has a similar, distinctive sauce accompaniment, while *rognons de veau* come lightly curried. There are fish dishes too – *coquilles Saint-Jacques*, or a simpler *saumon frais cru aux herbes* (fresh raw salmon in herbs, with a side salad).

The desserts, while not so elaborate, won't disappoint you – the classic *tarte tatin*, *poire au vin* (or *à la Chartreuse!*) or a *gâteau de chocolat* in a *crème anglaise* should round off an exceptional meal. Wash it all down with one of their moderately priced bottles of Loire wines – the crisp Touraine Sauvignon, for example – and you'll still have change from 150F. And to eat food like this, at prices like these, most people would sit on orange-boxes in the street!

DELUXE

Aux Crus de Bourgogne
Map Ref: 2C

3 Rue Bachaumont (Mᵒ *Sentier*)
Tel: 42.33.48.24
Open: lunch and dinner until 22.00
Closed: Sunday, Monday
À la carte: 130–150F
Wine: from 55F (bottle)
Service: 15%

When you encounter the 'uniform' of old-style French restaurants – varnished paintwork, yellow-cream unwashed walls and ceilings, brass rails, red check table-cloths and acres of mirrors – you can bet that the food will be rich and traditional. This place, tucked away behind Les Halles, and very popular with the younger, '*branché*' set, is a good example. Burgundy cuisine with heavy wine sauces is the order of the day: in the *coq au Brouilly* the chicken is almost gamy in colour and flavour; the *poularde aux morilles fraîches* (fattened hen with wild mushrooms, served with rice) is milder, and the mushrooms themselves, black, knobbly and full of flavour, are intriguing.

Other delights on their short, concise menu include *lotte à l'américaine* (monkfish), *ris de veau* (veal sweetbreads, a delicacy we have yet to work up to), *canard aux pâtes fraîches* (duck with fresh pasta) and fillet of beef in a Béarnaise sauce. Wine is not cheap here – 55F for the cheapest bottle, rising to a maximum of 95F – so for three courses of this substantial fare, in an extremely, lively, vibrant atmosphere, you'll come out at around the top of our range.

Dona Flor
Map Ref: 2D

10 Rue Dussoubs (Mᵒ *Étienne-Marcel*)
Tel: 42.36.46.55
Open: dinner only until 02.00
Closed: Monday
À la carte: 150–170F
Wine: 25F (50cl)
Service: included
Credit cards: Visa

Possibly Paris's most chic and stylish Brazilian restaurant, Dona Flor (next to the crazy *Fitzcarraldo* bar – see p. 51) is a notch above other South American eating-places we've sampled. But then the prices reflect that. Still, one can limit the damage substantially by missing out on the entrées which, although interesting, are quite expensive. And main courses alone make a substantial meal, with their side-bowls of rice, kidney-beans and manioc.

Possibly the star of the menu is the amazing *feijoada*, a Brazilian version of *cassoulet* with huge slices of spicy sausage and pork in an enormous tureen of sauce, all served with rice and an orange-and-cabbage side-dish. Pork figures too in the superb *carré de porc à la crème de haricots et aux choux verts* – tender slices of pork cooked with a tomato sauce, topped with cabbage and served with puréed kidney-beans, rice and manioc. Another front-runner for meat-eaters is the famous *churrascos* – charcoal-grilled beef or pork *à la mode 'gauchos'*.

For fish-lovers there's *camarões de bahia* (prawns), *crabe au laid de coco et a l'huile de palme* (crab cooked in coconut milk and palm-oil), and some other extraordinary combinations: *vatapa* (turbot with a creamy fish sauce); a *pot-au-feu de poissons*, cooked with tropical vegetables; and chicken in a shrimp sauce. Superb, imaginative cooking you won't find anywhere else.

On the alcohol front, the house rosé makes a very satisfactory foil to all this, particularly in the summer months, but for a little bit more you could treat yourself to a mellow Portuguese Dão, or a fresh, slightly *pétillant* Vinho Verde.

Then there's the *coup de grâce*, a range of desserts either based on coconut or combining exotic fruits (*sorbet de mangue* – mmm!). Star for our money is the *cochinos Dona Flor*, an extraordinary, almost indescribable *assiette* of five colourful desserts, combining such flavours and ingredients as orange, lemon and caramel with shredded, crystallized coconut. Quite the most unusual and intriguing dessert to come our way. Dona Flor – *magnifico*!

Le Vaudeville   **Map Ref: 2E**

29 Rue Vivienne (Mᵒ *Bourse*)
Tel: 42.33.39.31
Open: lunch and dinner until 02.00
À la carte: 140–160F
Wine: 30F (50cl)
Service: 15%
Credit cards: Visa, American Express, Diners' Club

One of a group of well known *brasseries* which also includes the

Brasserie Flo (10A) and **Terminus Nord** (10C). (For a full description of the food and style see those entries.) Run by the same company, they differ only in décor and ambience, the food and prices being roughly the same. As a result they tend to share the same strengths and weaknesses – the same crowded, hectic atmosphere, impeccable décor and service, and slightly predictable menu (once you've eaten in one or two, that is). Still they have very extensive opening hours, reliable, substantial food (the *lapereau de moutarde* is really good here), a great bone-dry house Riesling, and they're all very strong in the sea-food department. The one snag, for our purposes, is the price. It's difficult to come out paying less than 160F for three courses with wine; and for the house specialities you'll pay considerably more. But for all that, you should visit at least one of them while you are in Paris.

THE BEST OF THE REST

Wine-bars – cafés – bars

Café Noir, 65 Rue Montmartre (Mᵒ *Les Halles* or *Sentier*) – a cheap, lively bar.

Fitzcarraldo, 8 Rue Dussoubs (Mᵒ *Étienne-Marcel*) – a cheap and crazy bar; wild décor of old film posters; heterogeneous clientele of marginals, youth and workers. Go at least once.

Salons de thé

A Priori Thé, 35 Galerie Vivienne (Mᵒ *Bourse*) – a tea-room and café serving salads, quiches and the like in this stylish old shopping-arcade.

Food-shops

Stohrer, 51 Rue Montorgueil (Mᵒ *Les Halles*) – a *pâtisserie* dating from the eighteenth century, famous for its *pithiviers* (flaky puff-pastries filled with cream).

3e and 4e Arrondissements

*Le Marais – Beaubourg – Île Saint-Louis –
Hôtel de Ville*

The 3e and 4e *arrondissements* contain one of Paris's most
beautiful and homogeneous areas, the Marais. Stretching from
the river in the south to Saint-Denis and the Place de la
République in the north, and from the Boulevard
Beaumarchais in the east to the Beaubourg in the west, this
area was originally swampy marshland ('*marais*'). In about the
twelfth century the Church started to build chapels and
monasteries there, alongside an embryonic Jewish community,
and in the late fourteenth century, following the lead of Charles
V, the court migrated there from the Île de la Cité, and the area
around the Rue Saint-Antoine became the centre of
fashionable Paris – the street itself, leading to the city gate at
Bastille, becoming a frequent venue for tournaments,
processions and fêtes. (It was here that Henri II lost his life in a
jousting accident in 1559.) Gentrification was further
accelerated half a century later when Henri IV built the Place

Royale (now the Place des Vosges), which encouraged the construction of other fine houses and mansions, many of which still remain.

But with the building of Versailles, and then the outbreak of the Revolution, the Marais went into decline, becoming in the nineteenth century an artisan settlement and in the twentieth a working-class residential area. With little local money to invest, the architectural fabric suffered increasingly. After the Second World War, property speculators began actually to pull down buildings and build cheap apartments in any old material and style, and it wasn't until 1962 that the Marais was declared a conservation area; the state put investment into restoring it to its former glory, and now of course it is a very chi-chi and expensive place to live.

Architecturally and historically the whole area has an embarrassment of riches, with the Place des Vosges as its centrepiece. The first public square to have been built in Paris, it is flanked on four sides by almost identical mansions in trimmed stone and red brick (much of it a painted façade, incidentally). But besides marvelling at its individual buildings, the main joy of the Marais is walking its narrow streets by night or day, soaking up its indescribable atmosphere, with its green, colonnaded courtyards, its street-corner turrets and bulging, overhanging walls. And, amazingly, an authentic social life survives in this historical goldfish-bowl, whether in the long-established Jewish community of the Rue des Rosiers, or the newly-arrived gay sub-culture of the Rue des Blancs-Manteaux and surrounding streets. All this rich variety is reflected in the culinary stakes, with a choice of *nouvelle*, vegetarian, Jewish, Vietnamese and traditional, making the Marais one of the city's finest *gourmand* areas.

For the rest there's the Pompidou Centre (the 'Beaubourg'), latest honey-pot for the holidaying millions, with its array of tacky, untalented street-performers in front of the main entrance. Just one tip: do not eat in the streets next to it – unlike at Les Halles, there were hardly any restaurants here before the arrival of Richard Rogers's hi-tech pipe-dream, so every single one is tailor-made for exploiting the tourist market.

And when you tire of the Beaubourg's brash modernism, or the antiquity of the high Marais around the Place des Vosges, there are less well-known treats in store south of Rues de Rivoli and Saint-Antoine – for example, the streets and courtyards behind Saint-Gervais and Saint-Paul have their own distinctive charm. Here too is one of the Marais' hidden gems, the Hôtel de Beauvais, at 68 Rue François-Miron. And across the river there's the quiet, almost village-like atmosphere of the Île Saint-Louis with its wonderful range of often eccentric, specialist food-shops in its central street, the Rue Saint-Louis-en-Île.

BUDGET

Aquarius   **Map ref: 4A**
54 Rue Sainte-Croix-de-la-Bretonnerie (Mᵒ *Hôtel de Ville*)
Tel: 48.87.48.71
Also at: 40 Rue de Gergovie, 14ᵉ (Mᵒ *Pernety*) *Tel*: 45.41.36.88
Open: lunch and dinner until 22.00
Closed: Sunday, holidays
Set menu: 36F, two courses, non-alcoholic drink and service
    included
À la carte: 50–60F, service included

This light, airy, refectory-style, vegetarian dining-room on the edge of the Marais has attracted a young and mainly female clientele. Although the cuisine is not exactly inspired, by choosing carefully you can eat well at a reasonable price. One good thing is that the menu doesn't force you to eat a three-course meal if you don't feel like it – you could have just a salad and no one would bat an eyelid, unlike in more traditional establishments where they'd think you were sickening for something.

There is a daily set menu which is a hot *plat du jour*, a dessert and a drink. Then there is the à la carte menu which is divided into three sections: cold dishes, hot dishes and desserts. The first consists mainly of different varieties of salads; in the second omelettes figure strongly, with a choice of daily specials, different varieties of savoury tarts being firm favourites. Our recommendation is to go with the special, starting with *crudités* at 27F and rounding off with *fromage blanc à la cannelle*, a heavenly brew of *fromage blanc* sweetened with honey and cinnamon. There's no alcohol on sale but the menu offers the usual herby teas, juices and coffees.

The atmosphere is relaxed and peaceful in spite of the lunchtime rush – perhaps because service is a little on the slow side. Still, it's a good place to nurse a hangover or recover from some other excess. It's smoke-free and you won't feel uncomfortable if you're female and alone. Expect to pay less than 50F.

La Canaille

4 Rue Crillon (Mᵒ *Quai de la Rapée*)
Tel: 42.78.09.71
Open: lunch and dinner till 23.30
Closed: Saturday, Sunday lunch
Set menus: 45F (lunch), 49F (evening), service included
À la carte: 90–110F, service included
Wine: 30–32F (litre)

This is a really pleasant little place – bright, airy, cool, and done out in a sort of neat post-'68 décor, with framed revolutionary posters, pix of Che and Marx and cryptic murals adorning the walls. The food is good too – not copious, but stylishly and successfully influenced by *nouvelle cuisine*. The unexpectedly large, rambling interior can get very busy at lunch, but any delay gives you time to peruse the menu and to write your own order on the pad provided. (Is this what they mean by the involvement of the masses?)

As well as some more common items, there are some intriguing little starters: chicken livers with grapes on toast; a substantial plate of *crudités*, with avocado purée and mustard-and-cream dips on the side; or *poire au Roquefort*. Quite inventive. Main courses too are more than ordinary: *foie au gingembre* (liver with ginger, accompanied by rice or purée of carrot); *coquelet à l'estragon*; or *filet Julienne* (a cold fish dish with *aïoli* and selection of vegetables). And the other poultry dish was a winner – *pintade au poivre rose* is a large portion of chicken, cooked in a sauce containing small crunchy red peppercorns, with sauté potatoes. Delicious. The wines here are cheap and interesting – we sampled an excellent white Chevigny (made with the Chardonnay grape and much better than the Sauvignon sampled elsewhere), which was perfect for a hot afternoon.

Desserts on the set menu are more mainstream – mousse, *crème caramel* and *compote de poire maison* – but for a small supplement (and of course à la carte) there are some tempting delights for those of a sweet tooth, such as the '*mystere*', an ice-cream, sponge and nut concoction.

Let's hear it for the kids of '68 – they can certainly hack it here.

Meloni   **Map ref: 3A**

10 Rue des Arquebusiers (Mᵒ *Saint-Sébastian Froissart*)
Tel: 48.87.94.12
Open: lunch and dinner until 02.00
Closed: Saturday lunch, Sunday
Set menu: 53F, wine and service included

On the fringe of the Marais, not too far from the Place des
Vosges, this lovely, friendly little place leads a double life – a
genuine schizophrenic amongst café-bars. At lunchtime it's a
quiet, sober, discreet little restaurant, with a cool rear dining-
room, and in the evenings it's a rather wild, unpredictable bar
open until the small hours of the morning. Take your pick –
both faces recommended.

As for the food, it's a solid and reliable place to eat lunch but
you take what comes, which is usually fine. There's just one *plat
du jour*, plus two other options – *onglets aux échalotes pommes
sautées* (steak and shallots with sauté potatoes) or *assiette
paysanne* – for the main course. You can eat à la carte, but why
bother when for 53F you get a choice of starter, *plat du jour*, a
dessert, and wine or beer. Certainly a bargain. Starters range
through *crudités*, *avocat vinaigrette*, *salade d'endives aux noix*
(endives in walnut oil dressing) and a *terrine de foie de volailles*.
The *plat du jour* when we were there was *côte de porc
normande avec tortillettes* – pork chop in a rich sauce, with pasta
twirls. Other regulars which Meloni's inventive chef produces
week by week include *poulet aux anchois* (chicken with
anchovies), *agneau à l'orange* and *chilli con carne*.

For dessert you can plump for cheese or *crème caramel*, but
don't pass up their superb fruit tarts – redcurrant and yellow
plum on a melting shortcake base, the day we visited. For a
welcome surprise of one kind or another – day or night –
Meloni is well worth a visit.

Le Trumilou

Map ref: 4C

84 Quai de l'Hôtel-de-Ville (Mᵒ *Pont Marie*)
Tel: 42.77.63.98
Open: lunch and dinner until 21.00
Closed: Monday
Set menus: 45F, 60F
À la carte: 80–100F
Wine: 7F (45cl carafe)
Service: included

Many of the old Parisian restaurants are indelibly stamped with the personalities of their middle-aged to elderly woman owners, and here is one of that type, a former haunt of local artists and writers, where Madame Rouby, the *patronne*, shakes hands with all her customers and greets the regulars warmly. It's a biggish place with three dining-rooms and the one on the right is decidely the most attractive, with donated pictures covering the walls. Casual customers, however, are put in the centre room alongside the bar.

At lunchtime it fills up quickly, so get in before 12.30 if you haven't booked, though you may have to sit there five to ten minutes before service cranks into action. Even then it can be a bit chaotic. The set menus are 45F and 60F, both good value but with more choice on the dearer one. Starters are orthodox: *salade niçoise*, *crudités*, sardines, pâté and *saucisson sec* (spicy sausage served with butter). Most of the daily specials when we visited were poultry – *poulet rôti*, *poulet provençale* and *pintadeau cocotte*, a substantial piece of roast guinea-fowl (more fully flavoured than chicken), generously accompanied by sauté potatoes.

The à la carte choice is slightly more varied than in other restaurants in this class, with three or four fish dishes (turbot, trout, sole and *coquilles Saint-Jacques*) along with the usual range of meats. The set desserts are limited but à la carte there are some intriguing possibilities, including two dishes based on rice: *gâteau de riz sabayan* and *riz à l'impératrice*. With a good range of wines from 25F a bottle, you can eat extremely well in the hands of Madame Rouby.

MODERATE

L'Auberge de Jarente   **Map ref: 4D**
7 Rue de Jarente (M° *Saint-Paul* or *Bastille*)
Tel: 42.77.49.35
Open: lunch and dinner until 22.00
Closed: Sunday, Monday
Set menu: 80F
À la carte: 120–140F
Wine: from 39F (bottle)
Service: included

A fairly conventional-looking place, with no great atmosphere, yet it offers consistently high quality cuisine of the south-west and French Basque country. In particular the set menu at 80F (without wine) is highly recommended – why eat à la carte when the selection here is so good? Entrées include such regional specialities as *salade gachoucha* (with hard-boiled eggs and anchovies) and *piperade Saint-Jean* (a *ratatouille*-like purée, but with egg, cheese and bacon). Also on the menu is an exceptional *soupe de poissons*, packed with mussels.

Main courses include *cailles à la façon du chef* (two very flavoursome, lightly sauced quails, served with sauté potatoes), *confit de canard* and *pavé grillé*. But this restaurant is perhaps best known for two specialities – paella and *cassoulet*. The paella (served for two or more only on Friday and Saturday) is distinctly un-Spanish in conception – much drier and less oily, lacking the saffron colouring, but rich in chicken, sausage and shellfish. And the *cassoulet* here is reputedly one of Paris's finest, but again served only on certain days – in this case Tuesday, Wednesday and Thursday.

After a third course of salad or cheese comes a tempting range of desserts which are also highly recommended, particularly the *profiteroles* (topped with hot chocolate sauce), the passion-fruit sorbet and the wonderful *gâteau basque*. With a bottle of their excellent Muscadet or a hearty Madiran red from the region, this entire Pyrenean extravaganza will only just top 100F.

La Calanque   **Map ref: 4E**

2 Rue de la Coutellerie (Mᵒ *Hôtel de Ville* or *Châtelet*)

Tel: 42.72.34.21

Open: lunch and dinner until 21.00

Closed: Saturday, Sunday

Set menu: 55F

À la carte: 80–100F

Wine: 14F (50cl), 35F (bottle)

Service: included

Fish can be expensive in Paris, particularly in specialist fish
restaurants, which is why this place, tucked away off the Rue de
Rivoli near the Hôtel de Ville, is such a good find. Its décor and
style date back to Paris of the Forties if not the Thirties and a
somewhat officious *patronne* presides over all at the front bar.

Although they serve meat here, fish is their pride and joy and
it comes at very reasonable prices. There's a wide and varied
set menu at 55F which encompasses a good range of salads and
pâté starters, as well as their excellently spicy fish soup. À la
carte you can dip into *moules*, herrings, *escargots* or *crevettes de
Norge*. For the main dish on Wednesdays or Fridays there's a
breathtaking *paella maison* – a giant bowl of rice, *moules*,
prawns, chicken, pork, squid, spicy sausage, all cooked in a
hot, peppery broth. Other temptations include salmon, turbot,
haddock, trout or sole with almonds, and *coquilles Saint-
Jacques*, cooked on a skewer and served on a bed of rice.
Alternatively there's the other speciality of the house,
bouillabaisse – an enormous bowl of spicy fish broth containing
an assortment of fish and shell-fish.

Into what small space you have left you could squeeze a slab
of *dessert du chef*: a light caramel mousse cake in *crème
anglaise*. With a bottle of mineral water and a coffee, the bill
for this marine extravaganza came to a mere 71F. House wine is
reasonable, and eating à la carte with wine would set you back
no more than 110F. Highly recommended if you're a fish lover,
but get in early or book.

Les Philosophes

28 Rue Vielle-du-Temple (M^o *Saint-Paul*)
Tel: 48.87.49.64
Open: lunch and dinner till 23.00
Closed: Sunday
Set menus: 75F, 106F
À la carte: 120–140F
Wine: 30F (50cl)
Service: included
Credit cards: Visa, American Express, Diners' Club

When the thermometer climbs and climbs, as it often does in Paris in the summer months, places like Les Philosophes come into their own: lots of salads, several fish dishes and a light, fresh style of cooking which is quite simple but with an interesting *nouvelle cuisine* influence. It is also much cheaper than most restaurants of its genre.

The 75F menu is particularly good value, featuring two excellently prepared salads for starters – *frisée aux lardons* and *salade de tomates et avocats* – and *filets de hareng pommes à l'huile*. Then there is a choice of two meat and two fish dishes for the main event: *steak tartare* (raw mince mixed with raw egg – an acquired taste!); *côtelette Spinoza* (one of several dishes here with the name of a philosopher); a superb *escalope de truite de mer à l'oseille* – thin, pink-fleshed slices of trout, in a lake of delicate sorrel sauce, with small waxy, boiled potatoes; and an equally accomplished *filet Julienne aux poireaux* – a tender steak of cod topped with chopped leaks in a cream and chive sauce. A basket of fresh, doughy *baguettes* to soak up the sauce, a *pichet* of crisp, chilled white wine, and the meal was complete. Well not quite, for despite a somewhat protracted wait, the desserts too were formidable: *tarte chaude aux pommes acidules* is a deliciously sharp, slightly caramelized apple tart; and the *œuf à la neige* (also known as *île flottante*) here is highly recommended – a creamy soft egg meringue topped with caramel in a cold *crème anglaise*. A great finish.

The bill for this delightful lunch came to about 97F each. À la carte, you could really go to town in the evening on their fairly lengthy, sophisticated menu, which includes such treats as *escalope de saumon frais, medaillon de lotte au fenouil* and *fricassée de ris*. And the dessert-list features the famous Berthillon ice-cream and a selection of tastebud-blasting *coupes*, such as *Coupe Virgil* and *coupe Socrate*, which made us wish that philosophy had been as much pleasure when we studied it.

Piccolo Teatro   **Map ref: 4G**

6 Rue des Écouffes (M° *Saint-Paul*)
Tel: 42.72.17.79
Open: lunch and dinner until 00.30
Closed: Tuesday
À la carte: 90–100F
Wine: 30F (litre)
Service: 10%

This must be the best vegetarian restaurant in Paris – though as you may have gathered they are a bit thin on the ground. First appearances are a bit discouraging – crossing the threshold is a bit like stepping back through a time warp because, like many vegetarian establishments, its stylistic development was arrested in the early 1970s and won't move on. Stone-rendered walls, pine tables and benches, large hippie cushions and tiled floor made us grit our teeth in anticipation of food in various shades of brown. We were wrong – the food was light, imaginative and pleasantly technicoloured.

The menu is divided into three sections: entrées, consisting mainly of vegetable pâtés, salads and *crudités*; eggs, consisting of – well, eggs; and finally a section dubbed '*gratinée*', a wide range of vegetable mixtures topped with melted cheese. We started with an aubergine 'caviar' with yoghurt and lemon and '*tendrement roulées*' which turned out to be small *crêpes* filled with cream cheese and a salad – *mmm*! Two *gratinées* were sampled: one with fennel, chestnuts, carrots and apples topped with cheese; the other with courgettes, spinach and mushrooms. Both were very good and surprisingly light, although the spinach concoctions had a tendency to run to mush. By this time we were somewhat replete – then we spotted the desserts, so we shared a wonderful strawberry tart (the raspberry mould looked good too). There's a wide choice of drinks including herbal teas, juices, varieties of coffee and *chocolats*, as well as wine.

The one jarring note was the service – the place wasn't busy yet we had to wait a while to be served by the one and only waitress, who doubled up as kitchen assistant. But at least you can be sure that the food is freshly prepared, and despite this hippie hiccup we still strongly recommend it.

As an alternative to dessert and coffee here, nip round to the *pâtisserie* on the corner of the Rue de Roi-de-Sicile, which sells the most wonderful almond concoctions, and then on to *La Tartine* (see p. 67) for a coffee or whatever.

Au Vieux Saïgon   **Map ref: 4H**
24 Rue de Tournelles (Mᵒ *Bastille*)
Tel: 42.72.53.87
Open: lunch and dinner until 22.00
Closed: Sunday, Monday lunch
À la carte: 80–90F, service included
Wine: not recommended
Credit cards: Visa

There are lots of Vietnamese restaurants in Paris, and although this is certainly not one of the cheapest, you won't eat better food anywhere. The restaurant itself is a light, airy *salle*, all honey and pink with a loyal Vietnamese clientele which returns for the authentic and fresh cooking.

Don't be too tempted by the prawn crackers and tiger nuts which await every diner on the table – the portions here are enormous and you'll be hard pressed to finish a three-course dinner. Start with one of the wonderful soups which come served in large steaming individual bowls – *soupe de bonheur*, the house speciality, is especially good, packed with noodles, beansprouts, salad, beef, pork, crab, and garnished with fresh coriander. An alternative starter would be the delicious egg rolls served with a generous portion of salad leaves and a hot spicy sauce.

The restaurant specializes in '*marmites*' – rice dishes cooked in a small casserole and baked in the oven. *Poulet au riz en marmite* includes chicken, giant *cèpes* and ham, and could quite easily be shared between two. In fact many diners depart from Western convention by ordering several dishes at once, everyone tucking into what arrives. The food is so consistently good that almost anything you order will not disappoint, and this is one of the few places where we would recommend you be adventurous and order whatever takes your fancy. Be careful though not to over-order.

For dessert there are sorbets and *glaces* from *Berthillon* (see p. 68), otherwise the list concentrates on oriental fruits in syrup which we'd advise you to steer clear of. The drinks are not particularly cheap and we recommend you go native and drink *bière chinoise* or *thé au jasmin*.

DELUXE

Chez Jenny   **Map ref: 3B**
39 Boulevard du Temple (Mᵒ *République*)
Tel: 42.74.75.75
Open: lunch and dinner until 01.00 every day
Set menu: 82F
À la carte: 140–160F
Wine: 58–68F (litre)
Service: 15%
Credit cards: Visa, Diners' Club

It's not widely known in Britain that the *brasserie* (French for
brewery) is originally of Alsatian origin, though it's a term
that's now used indiscriminately for any large bar serving food.
Chez Jenny, however, is the real thing and well worth a visit.
Looking like any old *brasserie* from the outside, it's not until
you walk through the door that you realize how enormous it is:
stretching back some thirty yards or so, it is very roomy with
lots of space between tables – something of a luxury after the
cramped seating in many Parisian bistros. The décor lays the
regional associations on a bit strong – waitresses in traditional
dress, woodcuts of Alsatian peasants and the like – but don't be
discouraged.

The menu is broad, with lots of sea-food dishes, but don't
stray from the set menu which is all you'll need. Starters include
an excellent *soupe de jour* (vegetable when we were there), a
colourful salad (*hors d'œuvres variées*) and a daunting pâté of
calf's brain. Among the main courses are trout (a staple fish in
Alsace) and a delicious *coq au vin* served with pasta to soak up
its rich mushroom, wine and ham sauce. But this being Alsace –
or a bit of it – *choucroute* is the name of the game. Three
varieties are served, including the spectacular pig's knuckle
variety (which looked more like half a leg) and the *choucroute
poisson*, though beware of this as it has a poor reputation. On
the set menu you'll be served the standard Chez Jenny variety –
a small mountain of *choucroute* accompanied by frankfurter,
slabs of pork, bacon and sausage. Wash this down with the
dependable house Riesling at 68F a litre (with classier 75 cl
bottles of other Alsace specialities such as Gewürztraminer or
Tokay at around the same price) and you won't have room for a
dessert. If you can slip one in, there is a range of spectacular
ice-cream *coupes*, and the wonderfully light *gâteau au fromage
blanc* (cheesecake), a regional speciality.

All this, with wine, will come to not much more than 120F, and you probably won't eat for a day afterwards. Our only quibble was with the service, which was slow and inattentive, though the food more than made up for it.

Chez Robert   Map ref: 4J
4 Impasse Guéménée (M° *Bastille* or *Saint-Paul*)
Tel: 42.72.08.45
Open: lunch and dinner
Closed: Saturday lunch, Sunday, Monday dinner
À la carte: 140–160F, service included
Wine: 26F (50cl)

Lurking discreetly in a cul-de-sac off the Rue de Rivoli, and behind an ordinary-looking bar (L'Impasse), is this wonderful little family-run bistro with a most inventive menu. The carte changes frequently, but making regular appearances are entrées such as *saumon marine à l'aneth et au citron* (sea salmon with dill and lemon), *pain de poisson à la Basque* (terrine of hake on a tomato base, served with tartare sauce) and several pâtés (including an expensive *foie gras de maison*). Another option when we were there was the *omelette arlequin*, a colourful slice of cold omelette made with cheese and tomatoes and topped with spinach.

The main course list goes on forever: *choux farci* (stuffed cabbage), *lapin forestier* (rabbit), several regional varieties of *escalope*, and *tournedos de veau à la crème de ciboulette* (veal fillets stuffed with vegetables, foie gras, and a chive and cream sauce). For those who don't like red meats there are some extraordinary fish and poultry dishes: *paillote de saumon à la menthe* (parcels of salmon cooked in mint), *cuisse de canard au vin vieux et aux fruits* (leg of duck cooked in wine and fruit) and the house *tour de force*, *pavé de volailles aux myrtilles* (stuffed fillets of duck and chicken in a bilberry and vinegar sauce). There are also less elaborate choices like *haddock meunière* (smoked haddock cooked in butter and served with fluffy rice). Wash any of these options down with the house Muscadet.

The desserts are equally seductive: enormous *profiteroles*, a good range of fruit and chocolate *charlottes*, iced mousse with orange, chestnut gâteau or *île flottante* (an enormous soft meringue topped with burnt caramel, chocolate and sesame seeds, floating in a lake of cream custard!).

For all this including wine (and there are some reasonably priced house wines in both 50cl and 75cl sizes for between 25F and 35F), with efficient, unobtrusive service, you could end up paying anything from 140F upwards. But you won't begrudge a centime.

Jo Goldenberg
Map ref: 4K

7 Rue des Rosiers (Mᵒ *Saint-Paul*)
Tel: 48.87.20.16
Open: lunch and dinner until 22.00 every day
À la carte: 120–140F, service included
Wine: 52F (bottle)

An institution, an experience, a way of life – Goldenberg's is without doubt the most famous Jewish restaurant in Paris, so famous in fact that in 1982 it was the victim of a fascist machine-gun attack which left six dead and many injured. Located at the heart of the Jewish quarter of the Marais, it combines an amazing delicatessen and food-shop at the front (salmon, caviar and blinis as far as the eye can see) with a homely, multi-level restaurant at the rear. It's a must for anyone wanting to sample the best of central European Yiddish cuisine, and it has the added bonus (?), on certain days, of musicians wandering among the tables; depending on your mood and their skill, they can be a great enhancer of atmosphere or a real pain in the neck (or ear). But bear in mind that Jewish food is not known for its lightness or subtlety; in our opinion this meaty, rather hearty food is best sampled in the colder months.

The menu looks more complicated than it is. Basically it offers three *plats du jour* which change every day, plus a number of standards such as *carpe farcie* (stuffed carp), *choucroute garnie* or *gefilte* fish, all at 55F. On Wednesday the *plat du jour* might be *bœuf Strogonoff*, *poulet Budapest* or *boulettes* (meatballs); on Saturday *chou farci* (stuffed cabbage), veal goulash or moussaka. A great winter favourite is *bœuf au poteau*, which is an enormous piece of beef in a copious vegetable stew. Starters are simple classics such as blinis and taramasalata, and if you have spare stomach-space for dessert after a Goldenbergian main course we would recommend reserving it for the wonderful halva, cheesecake or strudel, which are specialities of the quarter.

If you do manage to tuck away three courses, and a bottle of robust house red shared between two, expect to pay around 120–140F; for atmosphere, tradition and a great cultural indulgence if not the finest culinary experience, that's a small price to pay.

Restaurant Curieux   **Map ref: 4L**

14 Rue Saint-Merri (M° *Rambuteau* or *Hôtel de Ville*)
Tel: 42.72.75.97
Open: lunch and dinner
Closed: Saturday lunch, Sunday
Set menu: 95F
À la carte: 130–150F
Wine: 23F, 25F (46cl)
Service: 15%

This Aladdin's cave of a place really is a curiosity, and surely one of most beautiful restaurants in the whole of Paris. Eating here is like dining in an exquisite antique-shop, its dark unpainted walls and ceiling laden with eighteenth- and nineteenth-century sculpture, clocks, chandeliers, plates, pictures, vases and giant wood-carvings. Bronze, glass, porcelain and wood gleam all around you, providing a visual feast before you even taste a morsel of the excellent cuisine on offer. In fact the décor is such a hard act to follow that you wonder whether the food can compete. Well it can – just.

The menu is short and on the fleshy side, so non-meat-lovers (except those more interested in *objets d'art*) had better stay clear. À la carte offerings include some fascinating salads (cress, mushrooms and Gruyère, for example) and various cuts of beef, but we would recommend the set menu at 95F which is very good value even without wine and service. From the salads our first choice was the *frisée aux lardons*, fresh curly lettuce with a generous sprinkling of hot bacon pieces in a sharp vinegar dressing. Main courses offered *tournedos grillés*, *andouillette lyonnaise* (Lyon sausage) and a constant favourite of ours, *lapin à la moutarde*. The bunny was a winner: an enormous tender leg, smothered in a mild, creamy mustard sauce, with the most delicious *gratin dauphinois* potatoes in Paris – sizzling, cheesy and crispy, straight from the oven in individual tureens. For liquid accompaniment the carafe of chilled house Sauvignon was perfect.

But the treats did not end there: the *tarte maison aux fraises* had been eyeing us all evening from a quaint eighteenth-century table near the bar, and we swiftly capitulated to its succulent strawberries, creamy custard filling and shortbread base which melted on the tongue. Overwhelmed visually, sated gastronomically, we left Le Curieux after ninety of the most pleasurable minutes we've ever spent with our clothes on.

THE BEST OF THE REST

Wine-bars – cafés – bars

Au Franc Pinot, 1 Quai de Bourbon, 4ᵉ (Mᵒ *Pont Marie*) – a wine-bar on the north side of the Île Saint-Louis, a cool place to drink or snack in summer.

Ma Bourgogne, 19 Place des Vosges, 4ᵉ (Mᵒ *Saint-Paul*) – an ever-crowded café-restaurant under the arches of one of Paris's most beautiful squares. One of Maigret's old haunts, but getting rather chi-chi these days. Still a great spot.

Au Petit Fer à Cheval, 30 Rue Vieille-du-Temple, 4ᵉ (Mᵒ *Saint-de Ville*) – a popular neighbourhood café still boasting a horse-shoe (*fer à cheval*) bar.

Quatrième Sans Ascenseur, 8 Rue des Écouffes, 4ᵉ (Mᵒ *Saint-Paul*) – a rather up-market café staying open well into the night. For chic insomniacs.

La Tartine, 24 Rue de Rivoli, 4ᵉ (Mᵒ *Saint-Paul*) – definitely our favourite wine-bar in Paris. Run-down, lots of character, great wine by the glass or bottle, open Sunday and every night till 22.30 or so.

Vins des Pyrénées, 25 Rue Beautreillis, 4ᵉ (Mᵒ *Bastille*) – a large old-fashioned wine-shop, frequented by locals, with a bar at the rear.

Salons de thé

Charlotte de l'Île, 24 Rue Saint-Louis-en-Île, 4ᵉ (Mᵒ *Pont Marie* or *Sully-Morland*) – the kind of shop-cum-tea-salon you hardly ever find in England, and one of the prettiest shops in all Paris! Its speciality is chocolate figurines, and tucked away at the back is a tiny tea-salon.

L'Ébouillante, 6 Rue des Barres, 4ᵉ (Mᵒ *Pont Marie* or *Saint-Paul*) – a tiny café/tea-shop on a lovely cobbled pedestrian street behind Saint Gervais.

Le Loir dans la Théïère, 3 Rue des Rosiers, 4ᶜ (Mᵒ *Saint-Paul*) – a tea-salon-cum-café just down the road from **Jo Goldenberg's** (4K), suitable for reasonably priced tea or a light lunch.

Food-shops

Berthillon, 31 Rue Saint-Louis-en-Île, 4ᶜ (Mᵒ *Pont Marie*) – home of the finest ice-cream in Paris. Made in many flavours, and bought by all the best restaurants, you can get it also from a number of places near by: *Esterina*, 88 Rue Saint-Louis-en-Île; *Lady Jane*, 4 Quai d'Orléans; and *Le Flore en Île*, 42 Quai d'Orléans. You won't begrudge the search.

Brocco, 180 Rue du Temple, 3ᵉ (Mᵒ *République*) – a classy *pâtisserie* and chocolate-shop where you can eat a cake and drink a thick, frothy espresso.

Chocaine, 7 Rue Saint-Merri, 4ᵉ (Mᵒ *Rambuteau* or *Hôtel de Ville*) – if you pass this shop in a hurry you might think it's just a chi-chi greengrocers. But look more carefully and you'll see everything in the shop is made of marzipan! A real visual treat, even if you don't buy.

Finkelsztajn, 27 Rue des Rosiers, 4ᵉ (Mᵒ *Saint-Paul*) – the best of the many local Jewish cake-shops, selling cheesecake, slabs of *apfelstrudel* and other such disgustingly delightful fare.

Lecomte, 76 Rue Saint-Louis-en-Île, 4ᵉ (Mᵒ *Pont Marie*) – a cheese-shop on one of Paris's most interesting streets for gastronomic delights.

Onfroy, 34 Rue de Saintonge, 3ᵉ (Mᵒ *Filles du Calvaire*) – a beautiful bread-shop featuring several *pains de campagne* and a great sour rye bread.

(*Pâtisserie X*), 30 Roi de Sicile, 4ᵉ (corner of Rue des Écouffes) (Mᵒ *Saint-Paul*) – our favourite cake-shop has no name, but we never pass it without calling in for one of their wonderful cakes or pastries. Just round the corner from *La Tartine* (see above, p. 67).

Paul Bugat (Clichy), 5 Boulevard Beaumarchais, 4ᵉ (Mᵒ *Bastille*) – a great *pâtisserie* and tea-shop serving snacks all day. Also great chocolates, such as the bitter *mendiants*.

5ᵉ Arrondissement

Mouffetard – Sorbonne – Panthéon – Port-Royal

Flanked by the Seine and the Boulevards Saint-Michel,
Port-Royal and Saint-Marcel, this area is best known for its
Latin Quarter and the university complex of the Sorbonne. At
its heart, towering nobly above the Left Bank, is the Panthéon,
one of the city's most unmistakable edifices. Originally built by
Louis XV as a church, it is now the national mausoleum for
France's worthies, though many of them are buried elsewhere
in the city. (Zola was actually moved here from the Cimetière
Montmartre, abandoning his wife in death as in life.)

But there are other, lesser-known corners which deserve to
be explored. One that has recently crept onto the tourist map is
the Rue Mouffetard and the Place de la Contrescarpe area.
Mouffetard, in particular, is one of the most attractive and
colourful street markets in Paris. It gets its name from the river
which used to flow there (now part of the underground sewer
system), used for over three centuries by tanners, skinners and
dyers who settled in the area ('*mouffette*' means 'skunk' or 'bad

smell'). Records of a street market around what was once the main road out of Paris to Lyon go back to 1350, though most of the houses date from the seventeenth century; one of them, at No. 122, still has the original standard of a former wine-shop, À la Bonne Source.

West of Mouffetard and south of the Panthéon are the narrow streets which figured most in the opening stages of the historic events of May 1968; the Rue Gay-Lussac, leading to the Boulevard Saint-Michel, was the principal site of those battles on the barricades with the CRS.

Today a Sunday morning rummage down the Mouffetard, lunch in one of the cheap local restaurants, and then a stroll or slump in the Jardin du Luxembourg, is a great way to spend the day. Eating around here is nearly always cheap, though on the street itself the ubiquitous Greek kebab joint has tended to take over. The same applies to the most touristic part of the Latin Quarter, the narrow streets and alleys off Saint-Michel: the Rues de la Harpe, de la Huchette and Saint-Séverin are now entirely overrun with Greek and Turkish restaurants catering almost exclusively for tourists. Our tip is to avoid them assiduously unless you enjoy eating mediocre food, being stared at by passing hordes and accosted for money by itinerant drunks. Instead we recommend two or three much more peaceful, reliable eating-spots just across the Rue Saint-Jacques.

The quiet side of the 5ᵉ is to the east. Over by the river is the recently created open-air sculpture garden, which makes a pleasant waterside walk, leading to the Jardin des Plantes by the Gare d'Austerlitz. One of the city's few substantial green spaces, it contains the Natural History Museum and what must be the world's most decrepit zoo, dating back to the nineteenth century, where the poor animals look almost as old. Still, they can't date from before 1870 — in that year, during the siege of Paris by the Prussians, all the zoo's inmates were eaten by the richer inhabitants of the city. Behind the Jardin des Plantes, on the Rue Geoffroy-Saint-Hilaire, is Paris's only mosque, part of which is a lovely courtyard where you can take tea (see p. 85).

BUDGET

Le Baptiste
Map ref: 5A

11 Rue des Boulangers (Mᵒ *Jussieu*)
Tel: 43.25.57.24
Open: lunch and dinner till 23.00
Closed: Saturday lunch, Sunday
Set menu: 48F
À la carte: 110–120F
Wine: 18F (50cl)
Service: included
Credit cards: Visa

A cosy, pretty little place with stone walls, wooden beams and homely provincial objects, Le Baptiste serves sound, reliable food with a few imaginative touches at extremely reasonable prices. The 48F menu in particular (without drink) is especially good value: pitch in with a substantial salad (plain, Roquefort or walnut), *cervelas rémoulade* (spicy garlic sausage) or the *tartine de Baptiste*, which is a curiously elaborate open sandwich – a poached egg on toast, on a bed of salad, all topped with an onion sauce. Certainly a novel combination, though the purists might squawk.

There's a dash of creativity amongst the main dishes too – *mille-feuilles florentines* is a flaky, layered pastry with spinach, while the tender *blanquette de veau* is served in an egg-and-cream sauce with a sliced, baked potato. Those with a sweet tooth won't be disappointed, either: the *tarte aux cerises* is a heavenly fresh cherry and stiff custard creation; and there's also a classic *tarte tatin chaude*, a *flan à la noix coco*, and *profiteroles* smothered in chocolate sauce.

In the evening, dining à la carte from a wider menu including some fish dishes, you could eat here really well for around 120F with wine, which makes it a useful standby for those on an average budget.

Chez Hamadi (Le Bouté Grill)

12 Rue Boutebrie (M° *Saint-Michel*)
Tel: 43.54.03.30
Open: lunch and dinner until 23.00 every day
Set menu: 59F, wine and service included
À la carte: 75–85F, service at 15%
Wine: 27F (bottle)

Most of the good, cheap *couscous* places in Paris are in the outer *arrondissements*, which is why this place just off the Boulevard Saint-Germain is such a find, and why there are often queues for tables; but persevere, as the turnover is fairly quick, and the wait well worth it.

The interior is small, a little cramped even, and hung with Tunisian pottery and *objets d'art*; service is rather on the abrupt side, but the food is copious and satisfying. There is a set menu which offers a simple starter, a choice of chicken, *merguez* or lamb *couscous*, plus a dessert and a small *pichet* of *vin de table*. But beware of the desserts described as fruit *en sirop* as this usually means tinned. Perhaps a better idea here is to eat à la carte which permits you to skip the starter, although the Tunisian speciality *brick à l'œuf* (a soft cooked egg and tender flakes of meat wrapped in a crispy, wafer-thin envelope of deep-fried batter) is very good here. Going à la carte also gives you the chance to sample a range of interesting Tunisian *pâtisserie* and to try one of the cheap (and rapidly improving) Tunisian wines. It won't cost you much more.

The main event is, of course, *couscous* in its many splendid varieties. You could go for the *royale* and sample all of them, though you'd get better value by plumping for something like *brochette de veau*, a veal kebab served like all the other choices with a big bowl of *couscous* and a generous vegetable stew. Vegetarians can eat well here, too – for 30F the menu promises a double helping of vegetables.

The best liquid accompaniment to this North African feast is a local wine, either the potent, heady reds, or the refreshing Rosé de Carthage which at 27F is every bit as good as its French equivalents. Also, try some mint tea to round off your meal – a delicate glass arrives at the table and the tea is poured from a silver pot held high above your head.

Les Degrés de Notre-Dame

Map ref: 5C

10 Rue des Grands-Degrés (Mº *Saint-Michel*)
Tel: 43.25.88.38
Open: lunch and dinner until 23.30
Closed: Sunday
Set menus: 48F, 65F
À la carte: 120–130F
Wine: 49–53F (bottle)
Service: 15%

Tucked away in a little street on the Left Bank, opposite its namesake, this quiet little place with a cool, dark interior and tables spilling out onto the narrow pavement is a pleasant place to eat at any time of day. It has two good set menus at 48F and 65F, the latter including some imaginative house specialities.

A nice feature is the self-service first course of *charcuterie* and *crudités*, with a choice of about ten appetizing salads which you sample and mix to your own taste. Main courses include *poulet aux champignons*, served with a buttered baked potato and garnished with salad; *coquelet forestière*; *pavé grillé béarnaise*; *kefte aux champignons*; *rognons d'agneau*; and the two house specialities, *gratin de poète* (ham, chicken, rice and mushrooms gratinéed) and *délice du Grand-Degrés* (ham, chicken, spinach and mushrooms). For something lighter, you could try one of the range of *crêpes* either from the set menu or à la carte.

Desserts are enticing, too: even the simple *tarte aux pommes chaude* was mouth-watering, and such confections as *le chaud et froid* (ice-creama and *crêpe flambée*), *vacherin maison flambé au Grand Marnier*, or one of their range of ice-creams should round off your meal with a flourish of pleasure.

MODERATE

Le Buisson Ardent

Map ref: 5D

25 Rue Jussieu (Mᵒ *Jussieu*)
Tel: 43.54.93.02
Open: lunch and dinner until 22.30 (23.00 on Friday)
Closed: Saturday, Sunday
Set menu: 97F
À la carte: 110–120F
Wine: 18F (50cl)
Service: 15%

Overshadowed by the dreadful blockhouses of the University of Paris, and close by the Jardin des Plantes, this is anything but a student haunt. Le Buisson Ardent is into serious bourgeois cuisine at very reasonable prices, and in its friendly, brown-panelled dining-room we ate some of the best food we've ever tasted. The four-course set menu at 97F (service and wine on top) offers excellent value, though if you choose carefully you wouldn't spend much more à la carte for three courses.

Alongside the standard French openers, the changing menu offers several slightly more interesting treats: a delicious leek tart; cucumbers in cream; and *feuilletté de Roquefort* (hot Roquefort cheese wrapped in puff pastry). Main courses (which are not large, but expertly cooked and served) include *châteaubriant à la sauce béarnaise*, *gigots d'agneau* and several other red meats which are carefully chosen from a market wholesaler who has supplied this restaurant for the past eleven years. *Confit* and *magret de canard* are regular features, while *cassoulet* puts in an appearance from time to time. The veal too is first class – *médaillons de veau*, for example, served in a creamy sauce and, like all the meat dishes, accompanied by wonderful *pommes de terre gratin*. And there are also fish dishes, which change twice daily. On our visit there was *merlan* (whiting) cooked in a light, mustardy sauce.

At this point the set menu offers you either salad or cheese before going on to the desserts. These include all the old favourites, but highly recommended is the superb *tarte tatin* (a hot upside-down caramelized apple pie). Ask for some *crème fraîche* – it costs extra but is the crowning glory.

Wines are very reasonable: as well as the house Bordeaux, served in 50cl *pichets*, there's a Côtes du Rhône at 31F and an excellent Muscadet at 37F which we shared among four of us along with a supple Côtes de Beaune Villages at 76F. Even so, our final bill averaged only 130F each, which for food of this quality must be one of Paris's better gastronomic deals.

Chieng-Mai   Map ref: 5E

12 Rue Frederic-Sauton (M° *Maubert-Mutualité*)
Tel: 43.25.45.45
Open: lunch and dinner until 22.30
Closed: Sunday
Set menus: 79F, 104F, 120F, 136F
À la carte: 110–130F
Wine: 47–50F (bottle)
Service: 15%
Credit cards: Access, Visa, American Express, Diners' Club

Reputed to be one of the best Thai restaurants in Paris, this relaxed, pleasant place serving excellent food must certainly be amongst the front-runners. The food is consistently fresh and well-produced, each dish providing a piquant experience for jaded taste-buds, and a real treat for those unfamiliar with the cuisine.

À la carte there is a wide range of choices, from sautés and grills to fondues and rice dishes. Of the four set menus the lunchtime menu at 79F is especially good value for a midday visit, when you can start with one of the house cocktails which come with the compliments of the management. In the evening, however, we suggest you plump for the carte and experiment. Start with something like *rouleau imperial thaï* – crispy, thin deep-fried pancakes stuffed with minced pork and vegetables so light and delicate that Chinese spring rolls seem crude by comparison. Follow with *brochette de lotte aux cinq parfums* (pieces of monkfish cooked on a skewer in a tangy yet sweet sauce), or *filet de canard au basilic et au jaune poivre* (duck in a fiery mix of basil and peppercorns), which also comes in beef, pork, shrimp and chicken versions, or our favourite, *riz sauté aux crevettes et saucissons thaï* – sauté rice with eggs and prawns, garnished with chopped dried ham. (Our enjoyment of this was, however, marred by the sight of it being heated in the microwave – black marks for this new Thai custom!).

We decided to forgo the puddings as they were somewhat pricy, and simply rounded off our meal with coffee. Although the French drink wine with everything, this was not, we concluded, the place to sample the delights of the vineyard; instead we opted for some excellent Thai beer, though you could go completely ethnic and stay with the jasmine tea.

This restaurant may be one of the best of its kind in Paris, but it isn't one of the cheapest, so study the menu carefully and order with one eye on the *addition*.

Le Grenier de Notre-Dame   Map ref: 5F

18 Rue de la Bûcherie (Mº *Saint-Michel*)
Tel: 43.29.98.29
Open: lunch and dinner until 23.30
Closed: Tuesday (winter only)
Set menus: 49F, 69F, 84F, service included
À la carte: 120–140F, service at 15%
Wine: 46F (bottle)
Credit cards: Visa, American Express, Diners' Club

Close by Notre-Dame, this place is something of a find for the hard-pressed vegetarian in Paris. Unlike most restaurants of its kind, its setting is distinctly up-market and even a little precious; but the food is fresh and wholesome, and if you're looking for somewhere '*plus chic*' then this would be a good choice.

There are three set menus all following the same formula of a choice between two entrées followed by a *plat chaud*; the most expensive menu throws in a dessert as well, although the other courses are so generous here you'd be pushed to eat a full three-course meal. The 69F menu offers a choice between vegetable pâté (a house speciality) and a slice of delicious savoury tart, followed by *l'assiette fermière*, a mix of rice, haricot beans, tofu, salad, chick-pea pâté and a vegetable *ragoût*. Served with an unlimited supply of *pain de campagne*, this makes a substantial meal. Alternatively, some of the à la carte choices look equally tempting: more than a dozen intriguing salads served in gargantuan portions, and hot dishes like *polenta*, *couscous* and a vegetarian *choucroute*.

The desserts are attractive, if a little on the expensive side: *fromage blanc aux raisins sec et noix de coco* at 31F, or another house speciality, *la crème de tofu aux fruits*, at 27F. Unusually for a vegetarian establishment, this place sells alcoholic drinks, the wine starting at 45F a bottle, as well as the usual herbal teas. Service is friendly and efficient and helped on its way by some English translations on the menu (normally a sign of some really awful 'international' fare, but thankfully not here!). Prices have risen recently, deterring the long queues which used to congregate outside, but it's still good value and now at least you won't have to wait for a table.

Le Languedoc Map ref: 5G

64 Boulevard de Port-Royal (Mᵒ *Gobelins* or *Port-Royal*)
Tel: 47.07.24.47
Open: lunch and dinner until 22.00
Closed: Tuesday, Wednesday
À la carte: 100–130F, service included
Wine: 30F (75cl)

Paris has many restaurants serving south-western cuisine, usually signalled in their name, as with this one. The food tends to be heavily meat-based – duck, pork, *pâté de foie* and sausages being staple dishes on the menu – and probably more suitable for colder weather.

However, at this fairly large establishment, which is furnished with rustic chairs and tables, the starters feature several fish and vegetable dishes like pickled herring with onions, which you serve yourself from a massive bowl left on the table, escargots, mackerel, salads, *asperges vinaigrette*, stuffed vine leaves and an excellent salmon terrine. Main courses on the whole tend to plough a more traditional furrow. The *cassoulet* had, unfortunately, been reduced to something resembling Heinz baked beans with sausages, and we can't recommend it. Other south-western specialities included *confit de canard*, *côtes de bœuf*, *châteaubriant* and *cervelles de veau*, and the chef went a little further south for an interesting variation – *poulet au riz basquaise*, which unfortunately had all been snaffled by the time we arrived. Fish-lovers had only salmon and haddock to go at. As befits a meat-based restaurant, most of the wines featured were red, with full bottles priced between 44F and 72F. On a warm night, however, we found the Rosé du Tarn most agreeable.

Desserts are limited and somewhat over-priced: cheese, *profiteroles*, sorbets and *fraises dijonnaises*. Our bill for three courses with wine and service *compris* came to 100F each. We were a little disappointed because the place had been strongly recommended to us by friends; and our digestions were not improved by a demented boxer-dog assailing us half way up the boulevard on our way home. If you're in the area, try it for yourself, but don't travel across town.

Le Petit Poêle   Map ref: 5H

12 Rue Thouin (Mᵒ *Place Monge*)

Tel: 43.29.41.93

Open: lunch and dinner until midnight

Closed: Monday

Set menus: 60F, 80F, 150F

Wine: from 55F (bottle)

Service: 15%

Another surprisingly good restaurant just off Mouffetard's northern end, with a pleasant stone-walled interior and tables out on the street. An excellent place for Sunday lunch when, unless you want to wipe out the rest of the day, we urge the superb 60F menu and caution with the wine – the supply here is generous.

Starters include *avocat vinaigrette*, *escargots*, *crêpe au jambon*, *crêpe au fromage* and the interesting *chèvre chaud* (hot, melted goats' cheese served on toast on a bed of lettuce). There is also an excellent range of self-serve *charcuterie* and *crudités* – potatoes with herring and the *tabbouleh* were particularly tasty. But take it easy, there's a lot more to come. Main courses are very meat-based: *brochettes de bœuf*, *gigots d'agneau* and the like, all served with salad and several halves of baked potato and *sauce Petit Poêle* – a tarragon butter for lacing on your bread or spuds. The recommended house speciality is the *délice de Petit Poêle*, a wonderful dish of chicken cooked in a cheese and ham sauce, with spinach, *ratatouille* and rice, garnished with a slice of bacon. Great!

Desserts too are substantial: sorbets, fresh fruit, *tartes* and *pâtisserie*. We opted for the *chocolat liègeois*, three scoops of delightfully bitter chocolate ice-cream, topped with Chantilly and chocolate sauce; and *chou-chou*, vanilla ice-cream with creamed chestnut, crowned with Chantilly (*mmm!*). The *Mont Blanc* omits the ice-cream and this produces a very sweet concoction – stick with the *chou-chou*.

The house wine, sold by the *pichet*, is reasonable, while bottles starting at 55F make this not the cheapest place to splash out on a classier wine. There are two other set menus: one at 80F, offering slightly more choice than the one we sampled; and a completely over-the-top 150F gastronomic blow-out, which includes a *salade folle* as an *hors d'œuvre* – a platter of *foie gras*, tarama, crab cocktail and smoked salmon, served with toast and a glass of vodka or Sauternes! Our more modest lunch, including coffee, service but no wine, came to 78F each. We thought we'd never eat again!

La Taverne

Map Ref: 5J

35 Rue Descartes (Mᵒ *Place Monge*)
Tel: 43.25.67.77
Open: lunch and dinner
Closed: Sunday dinner
Set menus: 61F, service included; 75F, wine and service
   included
Wine: 36F (bottle)
Credit cards: Access, Visa, American Express

Among the dozens of eating-places around Mouffetard and
Contrescarpe, here's a reliable and honest one which we
heartily recommend – its set menus may be a few francs more
than those being brandished around it, but remember the price
here is for four courses. The two set menus differ only in the
inclusion of a half bottle of the very acceptable house wine (and
a confusing range of supplements for certain dishes on the
cheaper list), so tailor your choice to your joint alcohol capacity
and the time of day. We wouldn't recommend eating à la carte.
   The décor is rather offputting for the purist – fake half-
timbering and 'Elizabethan' lampshades – but the service is
friendly and attentive. Starters include an excellent *avocat
crabe*, which is a whole avocado packed with crab in a
mayonnaise sauce; *moules* cooked in garlic butter and served in
a little *coquelette* tray; plus the usual range of salads and pâtés.
Main courses too are quite varied and interesting for this
standard of place, with fish dishes such as a spicy *coquilles
Saint-Jacques*, served in a shallow tureen with rice, or an
inventive *lotte au vin rouge*. Carnivores will like the *sauté
d'agneau aux aubergines*, which comes in a small brass pan –
enormous amounts of tender lamb in a thick tomato sauce, with
a whole aubergine sliced on top. Very filling. Alternatively you
could plump for *steak au poivre* or the *andouillette* (spicy
sausage served with salad and a large baked potato).
   After the cheese course we recommend the superb *pruneaux
au vin*, the enormous *meringue glacée à la Chantilly* or one of
the sorbet concoctions such as '*le Colonel*', which is a tart
lemon sorbet drenched in vodka. A nice sharp finish to an
excellent, cheap meal.

Villars Palace

Map ref: 5K

6–8 Rue Descartes (M° *Maubert-Mutualité* or *Cardinal
    Lemoine*)

Tel: 43.26.39.08

Open: lunch and dinner until 22.15

Closed: Saturday lunch

Set menus: 70F, 95F, 155F

À la carte: not recommended

Wine: from 45F (bottle)

Service: 15%

Credit cards: Visa

This establishment is actually two fish restaurants in one – a
cheaper, more relaxed place known as Petit Villar, and Villars
Palace proper which is much grander and specializes in salmon
dishes. You enter both via a single entrance, and then veer left
to the Palace or right to the Petit Villar. We got very confused
when we first ate here, but if you do end up in the wrong place
the management don't seem to mind the criss-cross traffic of
bewildered customers.

  In both places the à la carte menu is on the pricey side, so we
suggest you stick with one of the three excellent set menus. The
food has clear *nouvelle* tendencies – islands of fish in sauce
lakes – so the set menus actually represent very good value for
this type of over-priced cuisine. The 70F menu is only available
in the Petit Villar and offers a choice of three entrées including
two fish terrines and a rather flat and gritty fish soup. Main
dishes are rather more robust. We opted for a *grillandine de
thon* – tender grilled tuna steaks served with really scrumptious
pommes dauphinois – and *petits rougets*, small red
mullets grilled and served with the same vegetable side-dish.
Also on offer the day we visited was *raie grillé aux capres* which
looked equally tempting. But the real surprise came with the
final course: after the rather subtle flavours of the previous two
courses the desserts positively exploded with flavour. *Tarte au
citron* was intensely lemony and served with an equally robust
raspberry sauce; and the chocolate gâteau was a delicious
mousse-cake in *crème anglaise*. With half a bottle of house
white, our bill for this light and refreshing lunch came to 186F
for two.

  But if salmon is what you're really after then pop next door to
the Palace where the two set menus will give you a feast to
remember. Here the cheaper of the two at 95F is especially
good value, tempting you with entrées like *salade de saumon*,

mousseline de saumon and a ragout of scallops, and main courses like *la morue fraîche au basilic*, *haddock au beurre*, *papillote de saumon* and, for a 15F supplement, *saumon Villars*, the house speciality. Because fish restaurants are not cheap in Paris, this one is particularly good value.

DELUXE

L'Assiette aux Fromages   Map ref: 5L
27 Rue Mouffetard (Mᵒ *Place Monge*)
Tel: 45.35.14.21
Open: lunch and dinner until 22.30 every day
À la carte: 130–140F, service included
Wine: 64F (bottle)

It is said that France has 365 types of cheese, one for each day of the year; a more reliable estimate is 180, but that's still a lot of smells and tastes to keep track of. A good way to come to grips with the subtleties of the French cheese mountain is by going to one of the growing number of cheese restaurants in the city which offer a '*menu de dégustation*' – a range of cheese to taste – as well as other hot and cold cheese-based dishes. The most famous is *Androuet* (see p. 43), but it has become rather expensive in recent years. For something slightly more humble, try this new cheese-shop and restaurant on the Rue Mouffetard, which is ideal for Sunday lunch after a trip around the famous street market.

Bright and refreshingly modern, with an entrancing window display and a shady, quiet garden and fountain at the rear (pity about the kitsch Alpine mural), L'Assiette offers a range of cheese plates to suit all tastes. If you want three full courses there is a range of slightly expensive cheese-based entrées, including *avocat de l'avesnois* (avocado with a cream-cheese filling – nice idea, but a little bland), *salade aux quatre fromages*, *le chausson avreyronnais* (a savoury, flaky pastry filled with melted Roquefort) and a more simple *tarte au fromage*, which is a reliable bet. Then there are the *plats* – five cheeses per selection, all served with butter and (inevitably) a basket of the renowned *pain poîlane* – and don't forget the red wine, which is indispensable for any real cheese tasting. The house red, Oiselet, is very well matched for the job.

The selections include *douceur*, consisting of five mild cheeses – a little too mild, we found, though the creamy

Seigneur de Coulogne was a real find, as was the Brie de Lorraine; *l'auvergnat* (cheeses from the Auvergne); *chèvre* (goat cheeses); *saveur* (strong cheeses); and the *plat personalisé*, where you select five cheeses from eleven on offer. (It's a very good place to visit in a larger group when you could 'mix and match' maybe three or four plates.)

In addition to the *dégustation* there are several special cheese dishes on offer, foremost of which is *la raclette*, where you pour hot grilled cheese, from a special electric toaster plugged in under the table, onto baked potato – very hi-tech trad! Other toasted cheese dishes include *le Brie au poivre sur rôtie* (ham on *pain poîlane*, topped by melted Brie) and *la pela savoyarde* (sliced potatoes, garlic country ham and melted Roblochon cheese).

If you want to go all the way you can finish with cheese-based desserts such as *demi-torteau au fromage* a light, dry, airy sponge-like cheese-cake in a thin pastry jacket; *dessert blanc à la crème de mure sauvage* (sweet cream cheese with blackberry liqueur); and *tarte au fromage blanc avec citron* (a tart of sweet cream cheese and lemon). Not a cheap way to eat, certainly, but a genuinely instructive experience. (A cheese *menu de dégustation* is also available at *Ferme Sainte-Suzanne* (see p. 85) and *Ferme Sainte-Hubert* (see p. 43).

Atelier Maître Albert   Map ref: 5M

1 Rue Maître-Albert (Mᵒ *Maubert-Mutualité* or *Saint-Michel*)
Tel: 46.33.13.78
Open: dinner only
Closed: Sunday
Set menu: 135F, wine included
Service: 15%

While *nouvelle cuisine* proper is now a footnote in the history books its influence is still strong in restaurants such as the Atelier Maître Albert. After the richness of most French food, some of the dishes here might even seem a little bland, but their lightness certainly makes an intriguing contrast.

Opposite Notre-Dame, on the Left Bank, with a plain, uninviting exterior, Atelier Maître Albert is a haven of discreet elegance for Parisian yuppies. There is only the one set menu at 135F, including half a bottle of wine (with service on top), but what a set menu! Four courses, with fascinating possibilities on all of them, make choice difficult. *Tartare* of salmon, a quail salad with soft poached egg, *soufflé de langoustines*, a fish sausage(!) and ham stuffed with marrow and cauliflower are just some of the starters. The red wine was a young and surprisingly round Bordeaux, which was perfect with the starter and a main course of *grenadins* of veal served on a bed of fresh, spinach tagliatelle. Other tantalizing dishes included a *mosaïque de poissons* and duck cooked in Gamay (red wine), which was much appreciated at the next table ('you can't get good duck where I hang out in Cincinnati').

The cheese course gives a simple choice between Brie or *fromage blanc*, which is a yoghurt-like cheese eaten with a spoon. And then there are some formidable desserts, including a range of sorbets and ice-creams, apple tart and *marquise au chocolat*. All served with great panache. You might eat better in Paris, or in more style, but you'll probably pay twice as much for the experience. This is not a place to just pop in to – you'll need to book in advance.

Chez Pento   Map ref: 5N

9 Rue Cujas (Mᵒ *Saint-Michel* or *Luxembourg*)
Tel: 43.26.81.54
Also at: 36 Rue Vivienne, 2ᵉ (Mᵒ *Bourse*) *Tel*: 42.36.60.69
Open: lunch and dinner until 23.30 every day
À la carte: 130–150F
Wine: 28F (50cl)
Service: 15%

New cuisine in an old setting is the keynote of this popular place, frequented by the richer students from the Sorbonne just across the road. Certainly most of the effort seems to have gone into the food rather than the décor, yet the tall, old-fashioned, largely unpainted rooms preserve something of a pleasing shabbiness. Its packed pine tables and leather *banquettes* are presided over by the handlebar-moustachioed *patron*, who prances about frenetically when he's not dispensing drinks to customers waiting to be seated; and one of his long-suffering waiters has the lugubrious walrus face of Ben Turpin in the silent movies.

Bags of character then, but what about the food? One of the interesting things about the much-abused *nouvelle cuisine* is that you never quite know what you're going to get – and not always what you've just had! So much depends on the initiative and creativity of the chef that a list of mere ingredients conveys little of the visual pleasure or the often subtle combination of flavours that might await you. On the evidence of one visit, Pento is a good place to sample the genre, and certainly compares favourably with the much more stylishly appointed **Atelier Maître Albert** (5M) down the road.

The house policy here is an all-in price for a choice of starter and main course. The first courses include *confits de foies de volailles* (chicken or duck liver pâté with toast), *effilé de rascasse à l'essence de coriandre* (hogfish in coriander), *moelle tiède sur brioche en beurre rouge* (lukewarm beef bone-marrow in a red butter *brioche*), and *légumes printaniers en feuilleté*, which turned out to be a very delicate pastry parcel of spring vegetables, something like a small pasty, in a cream sauce. Then between courses a nice touch – a small, ice-cold kir sorbet on the house, to clean the palate.

Some of the main courses are fascinatingly inscrutable: *aiguillette de canard au parfum églantine* (wing of duck scented with eglantine); *carpaccio de thon* (tuna); *bœuf à l'orange avec des pâtes fraîches* (beef with orange and pasta); *truite du lac à l'oseille et aux tomates* (freshwater trout with sorrel and tomatoes); *lapin gourmand au basilic* (rabbit in basil sauce); and so on. None of these labels prepares you for the form or style of presentation – for example, *camaïeu de volaille au fenouil* is slices of chicken breast interspersed with slices of fennel, in a creamy sauce with little islands of a coarsely puréed mixture of what could be swede, cabbage and potato. A deliciously mysterious eating experience.

The house white is a pleasant, spicy Sauvignon *en carafe* – but Pento is the kind of place where you might splash out a little more on wine from their reasonably priced list, to complement the subtlety of their cooking.

However, the most visually entrancing part of the meal was yet to come: amongst the sorbets, mousses, 'iced soufflés' and 'soupes de fruits', the *mont de merveilles* (mountain of wonders) turned out to be an extraordinary example of *nouvelle cuisine*'s playful extravagance. Clearly inspired by neolithic burial sites, it consisted of a lake of custard and strawberry sauce round which were carefully stood fresh strawberries, cut in half, supporting a circular 'roof' of shortbread pastry! A memorable construction which tasted good too.

For this curious and often intriguing culinary experience, you will be charged around 140F, including service. You may not come away bloated, but you don't go to Pento to stoke up. For something very different, go, look, taste and wonder.

THE BEST OF THE REST

Wine-bars – cafés – bars

Le Bar des Carmes, 32 Rue des Carmes (*Mᵒ Maubert-Mutualité* or *Cardinal Lemoine*) – a traditional café-bar where you can also eat cheaply. Open from 5.00 a.m. if you're really desperate.

La Bourgogne, 144 Rue Mouffetard (Mᵒ *Censier-Daubenton* or *Gobelins*) – a pleasant local wine-bar with pavement tables at the bottom end of the Mouffetard.

Café de la Nouvelle Marie, 19 Rue des Fosses-Saint-Jacques (Mᵒ *Luxembourg*) – an old-style café for a drink or cheap eats close to the Panthéon. Great wines from Touraine.

Café Mouffetard, 116 Rue Mouffetard (Mᵒ *Place Monge*) – a popular little café at the heart of the street market. Munch one of their delicious home-made *brioches* or *croissants* and watch the world go by.

Le Piano Vache, 8 Rue Laplace (Mᵒ *Maubert-Mutualité*) – a cool, intimate and tranquil little bar.

Salons de thé

La Mosquée de Paris, 1 Rue Daubenton (Mᵒ *Censier-Daubenton*) – one of Paris's most exotic locations for a glass of mint tea and a pastry. Part of a lovely mosque built in 1922, there's a shaded courtyard with a tinkling fountain in summer, and an elaborate, imposing tea-room in winter.

Food-shops

Boulangerie Perruche, 68 Rue Cardinal-Lemoine (Mᵒ *Cardinal Lemoine*) – an ordinary-looking bread-shop making and selling a superb *baguette de campagne* which is streets ahead of the banal white version.

Ferme Sainte-Suzanne, 4 Rue des Fosses-Saint-Jacques (Mᵒ *Luxembourg*) – a sweet little cheese-shop with restaurant at the rear featuring a good *menu de dégustation* (see review of **L'Assiette aux Fromages**, 5L).

Lerch, 4 Rue Cardinal-Lemoine (Mᵒ *Cardinal Lemoine*) – a famous *pâtisserie* almost opposite the renowned (and expensive) Tour d'Argent restaurant. Celebrated *kugelhopfs* (coffee cakes) and *madeleines* of Proust fame.

Le Moule à Gâteau, 111 Rue Mouffetard (Mᵒ *Censier-Daubenton*) – one of a Paris-wide chain specializing in simple but succulent regional cakes and pastries. With *Les Panetons* next door, this is a great food-shopping spot.

Les Panetons, 113 Rue Mouffetard (Mᵒ *Censier-Daubenton*) – a wonderful bread-shop serving a varied range of fresh breads and cakes.

Ray Evans

6ᵉ Arrondissement

Saint-Germain-des-Prés – Odéon – Luxembourg

Extending from the Boulevard du Montparnasse to the river, the 6ᵉ is the heart of the fashionable Left Bank, with the Boulevard Saint-Germain as the focus of the café society for which Paris is famed. But it's also an area steeped in a history which goes back far beyond the introduction of coffee, and in areas such as the Odéon and the Rue Bonaparte, the historical associations are legion. The Rue Monsieur-le-Prince, for example, has a plaque on virtually every house announcing a famous resident, amongst them Blaise Pascal.

To the south, of course, is the Jardin du Luxembourg, one of the few parks within the city and a mecca for joggers – most of them seem to be American imports. But beware of a bizarre and ludicrous regulation – '*Pelouse Interdite*' – no sitting on the grass, anywhere; on very hot days it's a mad scramble for the upright chairs that litter the gardens. Almost opposite is the

famous Théâtre de l'Odéon, dating from 1808, the site of a
famous student occupation in 1968 when Roman helmets from
the props store were handed out for protection in the real
street-theatre on the barricades outside.

The Boulevard Saint-Germain has been well-trodden by
most of us, though to sit out in the street cafés is now absurdly
pricey. If you stay off the main drag, eating well is relatively
easy, if not always very cheap, as our wide range of choices
testifies. And there are some lesser-known historical gems here
too – one of them, the restaurant Le Procope (13 Rue de
l'Ancienne-Comédie) is the city's oldest café, dating from
1686. It was here that Diderot, Danton and Marat pondered
and schemed in the late eighteenth century; but these days,
despite its faded splendour, history is costing just a little too
much for us to be able to recommend it. Almost next door are
the Cours de Commerce-Saint-André and de Rohan, backing
onto the Rue Saint-André-des-Arts. This authentic, unspoilt
little passageway has some sombre associations with the
French Revolution – at No. 8 Marat had his printing-press, and
at No. 9 lived Dr Guillotin whose famous invention made such
an impression on the French monarchy and on so many of
Marat's contemporaries.

Saint Germain-des-Prés itself was established as an abbey in
the sixth century, and it exercised a powerful intellectual
influence throughout the Middle Ages – a torch taken up by
secular intellectuals in the surrounding streets and cafés from
the eighteenth century onwards. But that cerebral spark was
largely snuffed out in the 1950s when the area started to
become the terrain of the poseur and the fashion-conscious
'*b.c.b.g*' ('*bon chic, bon genre*' – the French equivalent of
'yuppie'). (The nearby street market at the Rue de Buci is
reputed to be the most expensive in Paris; it's certainly the only
one where a stall-holder has tried to swindle us.) The church
itself – the most significant building in Paris predating Notre-
Dame – with its eleventh-century tower and primitive
Romanesque interior, is worth a visit, and many of the
surrounding streets – the Rues Jacob, Bonaparte and de Seine
– have a centuries-old charisma despite the ever-present
bombardment of traffic. Right behind Saint-Germain is the
charming Place Furstemberg with its beautiful trees and on one
side the Musée Delacroix, home of the painter for the last six
years of his life. Less tranquil are the memories that haunt the
corner of the Rue de l'Abbaye and the Rue Bonaparte, just by
the church itself: there, in September 1792, during the Reign of
Terror following the Revolution, over 160 people were

summarily executed, hacked and stabbed to death by two rows of zealous Republican citizens.

One last romantic image of the 6ᵉ – our favourite bridge over the Seine, the Pont des Arts footbridge, in front of the Institut de France. For a special glimpse of this city's incomparable beauty, stroll across it on a warm, balmy night, wooden boards clattering and water gliding underfoot, the Île de la Cité, Notre-Dame and the Hôtel de Ville visible on one side, the Louvre, the Grand Palais, the Musée d'Orsay and the Tour Eiffel glowing on the other. *Magnifique*!

The Cafés of Saint-Germain

From the late nineteenth century until after the Second World War, French (and international) political, literary and artistic life revolved around a cluster of bars and cafés in Saint-Germain and Montparnasse (see 14ᵉ *Arrondissement* p. 146). These are now very chic and expensive places to drink and eat, and normally wouldn't be included in a guide such as this, but in case your romantic sense gets the better of your financial acumen, here's a run-down of who drank where and when, and a current assessment of these famous watering-holes. Wherever you choose, pull up *one* drink, make it last the night, and either watch the passing clientele or conjure up the legendary *habitués* of yore. In general painters and politicos tended to hang out in Montparnasse, while writers and philosophers preferred the heady heights of Saint-Germain, though real topers like Hemingway seemed to be everywhere.

Les Deux Magots, 170 Boulevard Saint-Germain (Mᵒ *Saint-Germain-des-Prés*). Established in 1873, and prestigiously situated on the corner of the Place Saint-Germain-des-Prés with two wide frontages for its rows of tables, it is now a magnet for street-performers, buskers and enormous crowds. In the late nineteenth century Verlaine, Rimbaud and Mallarmé hung out here, and after the First World War it was reputed to be the birthplace of Surrealism, with Breton, Desnos, Artaud, Saint-Éxupery, Picasso and Giacometti as regular *habitués*. Hemingway put in an appearance in the Twenties, to drink and read his poetry aloud, but the most constant customers were Jean-Paul Sartre and Simone de Beauvoir, who came to write for a couple of hours each morning throughout the Fifties.

Café Flore, 172 Boulevard Saint-Germain (Mᵒ *Saint-Germain-*

des-Prés). Less imposing and more cramped than its close rival, and with a very, very gay rendezvous upstairs, it was opened in 1890, Picasso and Apollinaire being early customers. It wasn't until the Thirties, however, that it gained a clear intellectual ascendancy over its neighbour, when Prévert, Sartre, Albert Camus, de Beauvoir and the film-maker Marcel Carné became regulars. The Second World War extended both cafés' artistic and intellectual reputation – when Nazi officers began frequenting the cafés in Montparnasse, artists and writers alike migrated here. After the war Picasso used to come here every night, sitting by the front door with his Spanish friends. In the early Eighties the Café Flore was sold for a sum reputed to be around £1.5m, on condition that it was kept the same; and in 1984 Les Deux Magots also went up for auction, quite probably fetching a lot more.

Brasserie Lipp, 151 Boulevard Saint-Germain (Mᵒ *Saint-Germain-des-Prés*). Right across the street from the other two, this is the city's most fashionable *brasserie*, serving mediocre-to-inedible *brasserie* fare (*choucroute*, etc.) at inflated prices. But the food is beside the point: people eat here in order to be able to say that they eat here, and the downstairs room is the only place to be. Although it's been popular as an after-theatre place since the early 1900s, it was the proximity of France's main publishing houses, Grasset, Gallimard and Hachette, and their famous writers on expense-account publishers' lunches, that put it on the map. Nowadays it's not so much who has eaten here as who you're likely to end up sipping Gewürtztraminer next to – President Mitterand often used to end up here after late sittings in Parliament, not to mention regulars like Yves Saint-Laurent and Bernard Pivot, presenter of the prestigious TV programme *Apostrophes*, with his guests of the night.

BUDGET

Millésimes   **Map Ref: 6A**
7 Rue Lobineau (Mᵒ *Mabillon* or *Saint-Germain-des-Prés*)
Tel: 46.34.22.15
Open: all day until 02.00
Closed: Sunday

If you don't want to eat a full meal, and would like to snack and drink good wine in a pleasant, friendly atmosphere, this little

wine-bar between Saint-Germain and Luxembourg is ideal.
Run by a big bearded friendly giant, Chico, it serves excellent
wines at reasonable prices – the chilled Morgon and a hearty
Vacqueyras were particularly good – plus a range of cold meats
and dips, all served with chewy, crusty *pain de campagne*. The
plat de charcuterie is generous, offering four kinds of ham and
sausage, but perhaps the most notable accompaniments are the
two dips – *tapenade*, a delightful olive paste, and *anchoïade*, a
tasty purée of anchovy. Both slip down delightfully with a
Côtes du Rhône or a Beaujolais. Before you leave, take a look
at the rows of witty cartoons in the front bar, all on the subject
dearest to this bar's heart – wine. And the slogan on the back of
the toilet-door sums it up perfectly – 'When cows start to eat
grapes, I'll start to drink milk.' For a reliable bottle of booze
between two, and a hearty 'snack', expect to spend about
50–70F each.

Restaurant des Beaux Arts (Cochennec)   Map Ref: 6B

11 Rue Bonaparte (Mᵒ *Saint-Germain-des-Prés*)
Tel: 43.26.92.64
Open: lunch and dinner until 22.00
Closed: Sunday
Set menu: 43F, wine and service included
À la carte: 100–110F, service at 15%
Wine: 36F (bottle)

Opposite the École des Beaux Arts, this is an unexpectedly
popular and reliable restaurant in a very classy Left Bank area,
good for lunch or a more leisurely evening meal. Its 43F set
menu, including drink and service, must be the most varied in
Paris – it offers a choice of eight starters, fifteen main dishes
and eight desserts! And the main dishes include some classics –
bœuf bourguignon, *poulet basquaise*, *bœuf gratin
dauphinois* (grilled beef with tasty *gratiné* potatoes) and *filet
de poisson* with *aïoli* sauce. Unlike the prices, the service (from
a squad of jolly middle-aged waitresses), portions and
presentation are a cut above the ordinary; for example, the
sardine starter was freshly grilled rather than simply turned out
on the plate from the tin, as in many establishments.

The hearty *bœuf bourguignon* – beef cooked in a rich red
wine sauce with carrots, and served with boiled potatoes – was
fine; among the other diners a firm favourite was grilled steak
topped with parsley and butter and served with a huge pile of

crispy *pommes frites*. Splashing out a little more
adventurously, though inexpensively, one can sample *coquilles
Saint-Jacques* and a range of seven other fish dishes, including
turbot, salmon, sole, monkfish and dorado. Poultry too is not
neglected (*cassoulet* and chicken) and other temptations
include *lapin à la moutarde* (rabbit in mustard sauce) and veal
cooked with mushrooms and spinach. While you would never
expect anything too sophisticated here, this charming place is a
welcome standby six days a week, and not just for the students
from across the road who regularly frequent it.

La Tourelle   Map Ref: 6C
5 Rue Hautefeuille (Mᵒ *Odéon* or *Saint-Michel*)
Tel: 46.33.12.47
Open: lunch and dinner until 22.30
Closed: Saturday lunch, Sunday
Set menu: 44F
À la carte: 100–110F
Wine: 21–31F (litre)
Service: 15%
Credit cards: Visa

Within a few yards of the hectic Boulevards Saint-Germain and
Saint-Michel, in one of the oldest buildings in Paris, is this
unexpectedly '*typique*' restaurant named after the beautiful
circular tower which adorns the corner of the street. Inside in a
low room replete with old wooden counters and battered
mirrors, at tables set in rows, the workers of the *quartier* gather
to eat good portions of traditional French fare at very
reasonable prices. It is possibly better for lunch than a leisurely
evening meal, though it is open until 22.30 at night.

La Tourelle offers a set menu at 44F, and eating à la carte,
with a half-decent bottle or a litre of the house wine, will cost
you around 100F per person. For the latter the house can offer
an excellent range of salads (including *niçoise* and *alsacienne*),
moules, sardines or palm hearts. Main dishes are, as often, very
meat-inclined: pork, beef and veal figure strongly, though the
specials on the day we visited included a tasty and filling *poulet
basquaise* (chicken cooked in a rich vegetable sauce, served
with rice) and *salé aux lentilles* (a slab of boiled pork-rib served
with lentils).

Desserts are uninspired – *glaces*, *fromage* or the ubiquitous
tarte aux pommes – and if you're eating à la carte you might be

better picking up a *pâtisserie* in a nearby shop rather than adding to the bill. But for decent solid nosh, in authentic surroundings right at the heart of the Left Bank, La Tourelle is ideal.

MODERATE

Indonesia   Map Ref: 6D

12 Rue de Vaugirard (M^o *Odéon*, *Luxembourg* or *Saint-Michel*)
Tel: 43.25.70.22
Open: lunch and dinner until 22.30
Closed: Monday
Set menus: 42F, 49F, 66F, 99F
À la carte: 80–100F
Wine: 18F (50cl), 35F (bottle)
Service: included

Hard by the Jardin du Luxembourg, in a fashionable and expensive area, this place is a great find. Run by a group of Indonesians and organized as a collective, it serves a distinctive variant of that country's cuisine. If the thought of collectives conjures up images of mayhem then you're in for a surprise – the food is well cooked and nicely presented by a group of middle-aged waiters and waitresses eager to please.

If you're unfamiliar with Indonesian fare then you'd be well-advised to follow most of the other clientele in choosing one of the excellent set menus which offer a selection of Indonesian dishes to sample, rather like a *menu de dégustation*. Each set menu is designated by a different title: the 'Melati' at 99F offers soup, prawn crackers, ten sample dishes ranging from vegetarian to chicken, beef and prawns, plus dessert; the 'Seruni' at 66F gives the same deal but with only six main dishes; and there are two cheaper menus at 49F and 42F offering a more limited choice. We recommend you opt for the 'Melati', though if there's more than one of you why not venture into the *carte*, and share with your companion?

The ingredients of the set menu arrive all in one go at your table – we sampled ten different dishes, each with a separate identity which refreshed the palate for the next offering – and the feast is served with rice to leaven some of the rich and densely flavoured dishes. When choosing from the *carte* remember that the hallmark of this cuisine is its use of coconut, peanut and spicy sauces; if you like this particular combination, then none of their offerings will disappoint. Old favourites it includes are *nasi goreng* (a fried rice dish with pork, shrimp and peanuts) and *gado gado* (an oriental salad with a sweet peanut sauce), as well as different kinds of *satay* (kebabs of meat or chicken cooked in peanut sauce).

Save room for dessert because the sorbets are an absolute delight and should not be missed. You are given a choice of two flavours from mango, passion-fruit, coconut, lemon and our favourite, ginger. Wine is available at around 35F, but why not try the fragrant jasmine tea as a non-alcoholic alternative?

We left after a pleasant evening thinking that collectives, south-east Asian style, might well catch on.

La Lozère   Map Ref: 6E

4 Rue Hautefeuille (M° *Saint-Michel* or *Odéon*)
Tel: 43.54.26.64
Open: lunch and dinner until 22.30
Closed: Sunday
Set menus: 61F, 70F, 89F
À la carte: not recommended
Wine: 18F (50cl)
Service: 15%

The majority of restaurants in Paris tend to draw their culinary inspiration from all over France, and the result can often be somewhat removed from its regional origins. Which is why this place is so refreshing. Part of the promotional office of the Lozère region (south-central France, west of the Rhône), it serves only specialities of that area, and even ships its crusty *pain de campagne* up from there three times a week! Good for either lunch or an evening meal, it's a place for serious eaters (hardly any foreign tourists darken the door, more fool them) who want to linger over copious, authentic dishes or sample the local wines.

There are three set menus which are all recommended – the dearer ones simply offer more choice. Starters include *soupe du jour* (a freshly cooked crunchy vegetable variety on our visit) or a plateful of the local *charcuterie* (hams and spicy sausages), all eaten with thick wedges of that delicious bread which you carve off the half loaf which graces each table. Then for the main course we recommend the *tripoux* (tender, mildly textured bundles of mutton tripe, served with crispy pan-fried potatoes) or the *petit salé* (a slab of cold cured pork, served with a lentil vinaigrette and a vegetable mayonnaise side salad). Other delicacies include *langue de bœuf, andouillette d'Auvergne, choux farcis, saucisse d'herbes* and (Thursday only) the delightful *aligot d'Aubrac* – creamy mashed potato with Cantal cheese. They also serve a range of omelettes including one with fresh *cèpes*.

Desserts too are a delight: after your choice of the delightfully creamy cheeses of La Lozère, including the famous Cantal, come the *gâteaux Lozère*, one a large slice of morello cherry flan, the other a large madeleine-like sponge smothered in *crème anglaise*.

This whole gastronomic tour, including a coffee and a half-litre *pichet* of robust red wine from the Tarn, came to 107F each and took two hours to eat – so don't pop in hoping for a quick lunch. But for something distinctive, satisfying and expertly prepared and presented, this little place is a Left Bank gem.

Polidor   **Map Ref: 6F**
41 Rue Monsieur-le-Prince (Mᵒ *Odéon* or *Luxembourg*)
Tel: 43.26.95.34
Open: lunch and dinner until 22.00
Closed: Sunday and Monday
À la carte: 90–100F
Wine: 10F (50cl)
Service: 15%

Polidor has found its way into virtually every restaurant guide to Paris by now, with the result that it's always packed with people queuing for a table (no reservations are accepted). But there's good reason for its popularity and it's still worth trying to follow in the footsteps of Ernst, Gide, Verlaine, Rimbaud, Hemingway and Joyce, all of whom have eaten here. Turn up early for lunch or in the evening and see exactly why it's one of the best-liked eating-places on the Left Bank. The answer, of course, has to do with its quaint art deco, lace-curtained charm and some fabulous, fresh home cooking at extremely reasonable prices.

Pick of the starters must be the *escargots* which are justly famed here, and then for a main course try one of the following, all cooked with panache and generously served: *pintade aux lardons* (a succulent young guinea-fowl served with curly endives and bacon); *canard de Barbarie* (Barbary duck); *rognons au Madère* (kidneys cooked in a Madeira sauce); *truite meunière*; *carré d'agneau aux flageolets* (saddle of lamb with white beans); or *estouffade de bœuf aux olives et vin blanc* (beef stew cooked with olives and white wine). Then you could finish with their superb *tarte tatin*, all hot caramelized chunks of sweet apple, with a dollop of cream, or *gâteau de riz au raisin smyrne* (a sticky rice-cake with raisins). Three skilfully prepared courses, plus half a litre of the house wine, won't set you back more than 100F. The only drawback is that someone else will inevitably be hovering for your table long before you've finished. But that's the price of fame.

La Porte Fausse   Map Ref: 6G

72 Rue du Cherche-Midi (M° *Sèvres-Babylone*)
Tel: 42.22.20.17
Open: lunch and dinner until 23.00
Closed: Sunday, Monday
À la carte: 110–120F, service included
Wine: 40F (bottle)

Close by the Bon Marché department store in a chic area, this place specializes in Niçoise cuisine and must be the best of its kind in the city. La Porte Fausse will satisfy the most discerning vegetarian, since many of the dishes are vegetable or egg-based; and unrepentant carnivores can also find satisfaction with the couple of fish and lamb specialities, although with vegetarian food as good as this, why not deny yourself the protein fix for once?

The menu is short but supplemented each day with half a dozen specials which can range from *pâtes fraîches au pistou* (pasta with a basil sauce) to *sardines farcies aux blettes et moules* (sardines stuffed with Swiss chard and mussels). Most of these dishes are served with a *salade mesclun* (a mixed green salad), and with bread, butter and a glass of wine would make an ample lunch. However, a good appetite should comfortably see off a *soupe au pistou*, a portion of *pissaladière* (a French version of pizza topped with onions and tomatoes) or an *assiette d'œuvres*, perhaps sharing one between two to start. For a hot main dish the cornmeal *polenta*, topped with cheese and tomato sauce, is a great Niçoise speciality.

The dessert list is perhaps the most impressive part of this menu, with really imaginative offerings such as *glace aux*

pruneaux à l'Armagnac (prune ice-cream with Armagnac),
mousse aux orange et rhum (chocolate mousse with orange and
rum), and *beignets* (freshly-made mini-doughnuts in strange
pasta-like bows and packets, dusted with icing-sugar).

The atmosphere is relaxed and cool and the service is both
friendly and helpful. All in all, a delightful and refreshing
experience. A good recommendation.

DELUXE

Aux Charpentiers   Map Ref: 6H

10 Rue Mabillon (Mᵒ *Mabillon*)
Tel: 43.26.30.05
Open: lunch and dinner until 23.30
Closed: Sunday
À la carte: 110–130F
Wine: 54F (bottle)
Service: 15%

Like many Parisian restaurants, this stylish, bistro-type place is
steeped in the city's history. Named after the master carpenters
and wood-carvers who used to frequent it, and whose museum
used to stand next door, it is decorated throughout with
mementos of their trade – prints, tools, carvings and small
wooden ecclesiastical furniture.

The food is a notch above the average – a wonderful fresh
ratatouille and an excellent *pâté d'Auvergne* feature amongst
the starters, while the main course list includes several slightly
unusual dishes often found in more expensive establishments.
The duckling with olives, cooked in port, is a superb
combination, as is the salted pork with lentils and the
andouillette (a grilled tripe sausage). Other dishes high on our
'to try' list include the stuffed cabbage and the *coquilles
Saint-Jacques*. There's also a changing daily special at a mere
35F. Desserts too are worth going for, the fruit tarts and the
wonderfully firm chocolate mousse being particularly
delicious.

The only detail to mar this otherwise excellent gastronomic
fare is the wine, which is not good value: no house wine, only
three whites listed, and the cheapest bottle, an ordinary *vin
rouge* or a mediocre Côtes du Rhône at 54F, is not a good deal.
Sadly this helps push this place into our most expensive
category.

Chez Maître Paul **Map Ref: 6J**

12 Rue Monsieur-le-Prince (M° *Odéon* or *Luxembourg*)

Tel: 43.54.74.59

Open: lunch and dinner

Closed: Sunday and Monday

Set menu: 140F, wine included

À la carte: 140–160F

Wine: 46F (bottle)

Service: 12%

Credit cards: American Express, Visa, Diners' Club

Another typical little family-run restaurant with regional origins, this time specializing in the cuisine and wine of the Jura/Franche-Comté districts of eastern France. It's a tiny place, with a slightly comfortable, middle-class ambience, and only seven tables, which makes it important to book. The welcome for everyone is warm and friendly and the food heartily authentic, though perhaps better suited for cooler days.

There is a set menu at 140F which includes half a litre of Bourgeuil red or rosé, and à la carte you'd be hard-pushed to spend much more than 160F, even with a bottle of the dry, full-flavoured Arbois rosé at 68F a bottle. As the entire menu is not very long anyway, on this occasion there's little benefit in not dipping into the full list.

From amongst the simple salads, *escargots* and the usual range of pâtés, the pick of the entrées has to be either the *jambon cuit du Jura* or the *saucisse chaude à l'huile*, a delicious smoked garlic sausage served hot. Main courses offer more variety and are the real business of the house. For the non-meat-eaters there are two fish dishes – *filet de sole au Château Chalon* and *filets de turbot sauce mousseline* – both generous fillets in distinctive sauces. Then there are the poultry specialities which are especially recommended: *canette de Barbarie aux olives* (Barbary duck with olives, for two people); and the *poulet au vin jaune*, served on its own (*pommes* or *salade* have to be ordered as extras, please note) in its rich Jura wine, cream and mushroom sauce, ready for mopping up with the copious, crispy *baguettes*. Other regional dishes worth trying are the *foie de veau au vin de paille* and the *filet de veau jurassienne*, both in local wine-based sauces.

For dessert the local cheeses are interesting, but the sweets are fairly mundane and unmemorable. Something which is distinctly unforgettable is the rare and delectable Jura dessert wine, *vin de paille* – if you haven't tried it, instead of a dessert sample a generous glass of this nectar-like, amber liquid, with its nose of almonds and honeyed finish. Sip it long and slow to enjoy the full essence of the Jura.

Restaurant des Saints-Pères   Map Ref: 6K
175 Boulevard Saint-Germain (M° *Saint-Germain-des-Prés*)
Tel: 45.48.56.85
Open: lunch and dinner until 22.00
Closed: Wednesday, Thursday
À la carte: 120–130F
Wine: 25F (litre)
Service: 15%

Right on the fashionable Boulevard Saint-Germain, within spitting distance of the **Café Flore** and **Les Deux Magots** (see p. 89), this authentic, reasonably priced restaurant in traditional style is a pleasant surprise. Still boasting its original décor (marble counter, cream walls, lace curtains, brown varnished woodwork and old, unused, gas mantles), it's a haunt of the local professional classes. (To give you a flavour, the night we were there one of France's leading medical experts on drug addiction was sitting at the next table.)

The food here is sound if not addictive – traditional bourgeois cuisine, strong on meat and poultry in rich, not over-subtle sauces. Starters are standard: *moules*, *filets de hareng*, *champignons à la grecque* (in a very spicy sauce), etc. Main courses are substantial – *cassoulet*, *canard à l'orange*, *pintade* and veal all figure. For something unusual try *cervelles meunières aux champignons* (lamb's brain with mushrooms) – extremely delicate, slightly sweet meat fried with mushrooms and served with boiled potatoes. Desserts are uninspired, though the *mousse au chocolat* is worth a dip. The house wine is honest, with more than a hint of fruit, at 25F a litre.

The whole meal came to around 130F, including service. You could eat similarly and cheaper elsewhere in the city, but for this trendy area it takes some beating.

THE BEST OF THE REST

Wine-bars – cafés – bars

Chez Georges, 11 Rue des Canettes (Mº *Mabillon* or *Saint-Germain-des-Prés*) – a lively, not to say boisterous, bar with a tiny cabaret downstairs from 22.30. A Left Bank institution for many years.

Chez Julienne, 40 Rue Dauphine (Mº *Odéon*) – a popular and friendly little bar, ideal for a drink or sandwich.

La Palette, 43 Rue de Seine (Mº *Odéon* or *Mabillon*) – an artists' and intellectuals' café-bar, perfect for a summer's day with its pleasant *terrasse* outside and lovely murals inside.

Petit Bacchus, 13 Rue du Cherche-Midi (Mº *Sèvres-Babylone*) – a wine-shop and wine-bar combined where you can sample three wines at lunchtime. An intimate place for serious wine-drinkers.

Salons de thé

La Tchaika, 9 Rue de l'Éperon (Mº *Odéon*) – a rather chic but cosy Russian tea-room that also does lunch and dinner. Great cakes, including chocolate cake, and *fromage blanc*.

Food-shops

Le Glacier Moderne, 55 Rue Saint-André-des-Arts (Mº *Saint-Michel* or *Odéon*) – a good ice-cream shop on this lively if touristic street.

Lionel Poîlane, 8 Rue du Cherche-Midi (Mº *Sèvres-Babylone*) – the 'daddy' of French *boulangeries*. *Pain poîlane*, an unforgettable crusty, brown sour-dough loaf which is famous all over the world, is sold in Paris in over 600 shops and served in 300 restaurants.

Mulot, 2 Rue Lobineau (Mº *Mabillon*) – a superb *pâtisserie* and *boulangerie*. Amazing macaroons, chocolates and tarts. An Aladdin's cave for those with a sweet tooth.

7e and 15e Arrondissements

Les Invalides – Tour Eiffel – Vaugirard –
Montparnasse

These two *arrondissements* in the south-west make one large
area stretching from the Left Bank to the *Boulevard
Périphérique*. Of the 15e there's precious little to say except
that it's predominantly residential, that it's Paris's biggest and
most populous *arrondissement*, and that it's bisected by the
city's longest street, the Rue de Vaugirard. Also that it contains
one of the city's most prominent but unwanted landmarks, the
Tour Montparnasse – surely the ugliest architectural blunder
ever visited on this city. Nearly 700 feet high – the inner city's
only skyscraper – its main merit is that you can ascend to the
top by high-speed lift for an elevated panorama of Paris (haze
permitting), though the vista is something of an anti-climax
because most of the city's major buildings are too far north to
be seen well from here. (There's a great view of the Gare
Montparnasse marshalling-yards, though!) For incorrigible
aerial panoramists, we would recommend the Tour Eiffel or
Sacré-Cœur as better bets.

There are few other spots worth visiting in the 15ᵉ. One is the newly established Parc Georges-Brassens, a pretty park off the Rue Brancion and the Rue des Morillons. Named after one of the country's most popular balladeers, who lived nearby in his later years and died in 1981, it incorporates some lovely landscaped children's playing-areas, and for the blind a charming '*jardin des odeurs*' of plants chosen principally for their smell. While you're down this way take a look at La Ruche, 52 Rue Dantzig, a superb round building designed by Eiffel in 1900, once the home of Chagall, Soutine and Léger, and now restored with a lovely garden full of sculpture.

The 7ᵉ *arrondissement* is something else again, containing as it does two of the city's most magnetic tourist attractions – the Tour Eiffel and Napoleon's last resting-place, the Hôtel des Invalides. We'll leave the latter to other guide-books, except to say that the vista from the front gates up the superb Esplanade to the Pont Alexander-III and over to the Grand and Petit Palais is a masterly creation of urban design dating from the early eighteenth century. Certainly an unparalleled delight to the eye, though as an amenity it is sadly under-used.

The same can't be said for the Champ-de-Mars behind the Tour Eiffel, which by night and day is one of the city's most lively and attractive spaces – *boules* players, joggers, sun-bathers, strollers and the overflow from the Tour make these woods, paths and lawns *très animé*. Perhaps the best time to stroll here is at night, when numerous football teams play games for money on the semi-floodlit central strip. But of course the main attraction is the Tower itself, which by night, seen close to in all its freshly-illuminated splendour, is absolutely stunning – floating and soaring, fretted and glowing, a lyrical testament to nineteenth-century technological optimism. The cheapest and most pleasant way of ascending, at least to the second stage, is by foot – well within the capacity of an averagely fit person.

The rest of the 7ᵉ is rather anonymous – expensive residential areas, blank, uninhabited boulevards, and all the pretty places hidden away behind high walls or in inner courtyards. To the north-east by the river, of course, there's the French Parliament – the Assemblée Nationale – and the converted Gare d'Orsay, now the Musée d'Orsay, housing the national collection of art from approximately 1850 to 1910, thus bridging the gap between the Louvre and the Beaubourg.

In culinary terms there's not much to be said for the region either – no distinctive themes or types of cuisine dominate here, and there are a lot of over-priced restaurants to mop up both the undiscriminating hordes and the rich residents. More than anywhere else in Paris, stick with our suggestions if you have to eat down here.

BUDGET

Au Babylone   **Map ref: 7A**
13 Rue de Babylone (Mᵒ *Sèvres-Babylone*)
Tel: 45.48.72.13
Open: lunch only
Closed: Sunday
À la carte: 45–55F
Wine: 6F (37cl)
Service: 12%

There's a type of cheap, old-fashioned French restaurant, usually family-run, which can be very off-putting to the foreign visitor – illegible hand-written menus, harassed waitresses, and bustling with a local Parisian clientele who seem to know the system backwards. This is such a place, but we urge you to persist because this is where you'll get an honest, square French lunch. Au Babylone is not the kind of place to linger for those classic three-hour French meals however; these days there are more and more French workers with neither the time nor inclination for such a ritual, so places like this are geared to a fast turnaround.

The menu is short, basic and virtually indecipherable, but all the dishes are good value and change daily: pork, veal, and beef figure prominently. And there are the usual frontline starters: herring, pâté, garlic sausage or egg mayonnaise. On the day we were there the *porc rôti* was pick of the day, served with a tasty and unusual lentil accompaniment, and the steaks were enormous and came with potatoes. Desserts are simple: *compote de poires* (stewed pears), *tarte au pommes* or cheese. The whole lot with dessert and a small carafe of wine or a bottle of beer will come to around 50F; without alcohol or sweet, say 35F. And you could be out in half an hour, if you wanted.

Le Commerce   **Map ref: 15A**

51 Rue du Commerce (Mᵒ *Émile-Zola*)
Tel: 48.28.77.01
Open: Lunch and dinner until 21.30 every day

For review and prices see **Le Druout** (2A)

Le Petit Parnasse   **Map ref: 15B**

138 Rue de Vaugirard (Mᵒ *Montparnasse* or *Falguière*)
Tel: 47.83.29.52
Open: lunch and dinner until 22.00
Closed: Saturday dinner, Sunday
Set menus: 48F, 66F, wine included
À la carte: 90–110F
Wine: 20F (litre), 28F (bottle)

On the longest street in Paris, and a *pavé*-throw from the ugly
Tour Montparnasse, this is a sound and cheap eating-place in
an area not renowned for such. The set menus at lunch are the
best deals here, with a free choice from the small serve-yourself
hors d'œuvres platter for starter. Alternatively there's a *panier
de cochonailles* (a selection of pork *charcuterie*) and two
refreshing seafood cocktails – *avocat* with tuna mayonnaise,
and salad with *crevettes* (prawns and shrimps).

Main courses, on the set menus at least, seem to be rather on
the meaty side, though à la carte there's *truite* and *sole
meünière* or *coquilles Saint-Jacques*. The *bavette* (skirt steak)
with onions and *pommes frites* is a popular, if ordinary, choice,
but there's also *brochette d'agneau grillé* or *escalope de veau
pané* (breaded).

On the sweet side the *tartes maison* (*pommes* or *abricots*),
which mix the fruit with custard, are very good and there are
several other tempting flans on display. And two slightly more
interesting and exotic offerings, à la carte, are the *pruneaux au
vin* (unexpectedly fine) or *figues au Calvados*. Friendly
and attentive service, sound staple fare, cheapish prices – what
more can you ask for?

Sampieru Corsu   **Map ref: 15C**

12 Rue de l'Amiral-Roussin (M^o *Cambronne*)

Open: lunch and dinner

Closed: Saturday, Sunday

Set menu: 31F minimum, wine and service included

Here's one for the politicos and all those yearning for the lost egalitarian ideals of '68. Named after a sixteenth-century Corsican rebel leader, this unique little bistro tucked away in the 15^e (not too far from the Tour Eiffel and the Invalides) is run by Claude Lavezzi, himself a Corsican and an International Brigade veteran of the Spanish Civil War. He's lost none of his militant radicalism, because here a genuine Utopian policy reigns – clients pay according to their means, above a basic 31F for three courses (including wine or beer). And it's all done on trust – you simply put the money, unchecked, into an open drawer as you go out. In each week's menu he announces last week's takings and expenses – a real example of 'open accounting'. Other restaurants take note!

An admirable system, but what about the food? Very simple, sound and generous. You start with one of two types of pâté or a tomato or cucumber salad, then for a main course there is grilled guinea-fowl, roast chicken, an enormous *boudin* (blood sausage), home-made *merguez* (smaller spicy sausages) or a hefty veal stew with green pepper, all served with either rice, purée potato or *petits pois*. And everything is cooked in full view at the front of the restaurant, which as you might expect is bedecked with political posters and liberation slogans. Finishing off with a slice of Corsican chocolate gâteau (less rich and more chewy than the French variety) – alternatives were cheese or a piece of fruit – I willingly coughed up 50F, a fair target for a three-course lunch of that standard in Paris. And if you too are tempted by this piece of socialism in action, please don't shortchange him (as about a quarter of his customers do, apparently, with tourists the worst offenders). According to his published accounts, he lost about 70F in the week before I visited. Solidarity with Comrade Lavezzi!

MODERATE

Café Max **Map ref: 7B**
7 Avenue de la Motte-Picquet (Mᵒ *Latour-Maubourg*)
Tel: 47.05.57.66
Open: lunch and dinner until midnight
Closed: Sunday
À la carte: 80–100F, two courses, service included
Wine: 48F (bottle)

And now for something completely different. This place is distinctly whacky and requires a certain sense of humour to fully appreciate it. Staffed, apparently single-handedly, by a sinister barman-chef who could run Bela Lugosi close for charm, its dimly lit interior is cluttered with all manner of ancient prints and objects (golf clubs, a stuffed merlin . . .). On each table is a bowl of French spring onions, which we at first took to be garlic to ward off the vampires. Still, its heavy surreal-gothic demi-monde atmosphere obviously exercises a certain attraction on the upwardly-mobile young middle-class of the 7ᵉ.

The food too is unconventional – the menu is short, and skips starters altogether, with the main attractions the *salade campagnarde* and the *salade de jambon et pommes de terre*, at 55F each. The *campagnarde* is an enormous bowl of mixed salad, deliciously dressed, with which you are given a basket of assorted *charcuterie*, two large dishes of pâté, a knife and fork, and left to get on with it on a help-yourself, biggest-stomach-wins principle. The second salad comes with a large plate of ham, but invariably Mad Max 2 is so over-worked that the piping hot baked potatoes tend to arrive rather late in the day (and why, oh why, do the French never eat the skins?). There are one or two other dishes of unknown pedigree – *choucroute* and *cassoulet* at 48F, *confit de canard* at 60F, omelette at 30F and *andouillette* at 45F. And for veggies, the large bowl of mixed salad on its own costs 30F.

Given that portions are enormous and supplies of delicious grainy brown bread inexhaustible, you can eat well here, with a bottle of Côtes du Rhône (48F), for around 80F each – 100F if you follow up with the cheese or *tarte maison*. For a very informal but fairly healthy meal in an oddball setting, Café Max has a certain *je ne sais quoi*. Just bring your own wooden stake or get out before midnight . . .

La Fontaine de Mars

Map ref: 7C

129 Rue Saint-Dominique (Mᵒ *École-Militaire*)
Tel: 47.05.46.44
Open: lunch and dinner
Closed: Saturday dinner, Sunday
Set menu: 57F
À la carte: 80–100F
Wine: 9F (37cl), 38F (bottle)
Service: 15%
Credit cards: Visa

We're thinking of running a competition for the most illegible menu in Paris. This place, with its faint hieroglyphic jottings, would be a strong runner. Nevertheless, crack the code – or ask – and you'll find that it's a homely place serving sound cuisine of a kind with which Paris abounds. And it's extremely handy for the Eiffel Tower, so when you've worked up an appetite climbing all those stairs, here's where to restore the calories.

Overlooking the arcade of the tiny Rue d'Exposition, it offers an ample 57F menu (excluding drink and service) which starts off with the usual trinity of egg mayonnaise, *charcuterie* or *crudités*, followed by either *tranche de foie* (liver) or *pintadeau*, a lean leg of guinea-fowl, served with carrots and peas. Then it's *compote de pommes*, vanilla ice-cream or *fromage* – a creamy, smooth Camembert-like Saint-Nectaire was on offer when we were there. Including a beer and a coffee, this fortifying lunch came to 72F.

Also on the menu, for an à la carte dinner, were *fricassée de canard* served with haricot beans, *assiette de saumon frais* and *gigot d'agneau*. And among desserts the *glace mystère* comes well recommended. All washed down with their noted Cahors red, at 38F the bottle, you could dine well here for 80–100F – but don't try climbing the Eiffel Tower afterwards.

La Petite Chaise

Map ref: 7D

36 Rue de Grenelle (Mᵒ *Sèvres-Babylone*)
Tel: 42.22.13.35
Open: lunch and dinner until 22.15 every day
Set menu: 80F, wine included
Service: 15%

La Petite Chaise is the main rival to Le Procope (see p. 88) for the title of oldest restaurant in Paris. Certainly the building it inhabits dates from 1681, and whatever the justice of its claim, this place offers much better value than its more illustrious, touristic competition. Also, its opening-hours make it a good Sunday or August standby. As befits its age the rooms are antique and tranquil, creating a relaxed and genteel ambience best appreciated at night.

The food itself is sound, if a touch uninspired, and the 80F set menu (with wine but not service) is fair given the location and general feel of the place. However, avoid the dishes with complicated supplements or the bill will rack up alarmingly. Starters are straight out of the kit-bag – *jambon*, *harengs*, *crudités*, *museau de bœuf*, etc. – though the *thon à l'huile*, a large portion of tuna with cold potato, was substantial and nicely dressed. You couldn't complain about the main course either – *poulet mentonaise* is tender, gamy chicken in a rich mushroom and olive sauce, with simple boiled potatoes on the side. This was accompanied perfectly by the nicely chilled half bottle of house rosé (note: only red and rosé come with the set menu – there's a supplement for white, for some reason). Other main courses on the set menu include *côte de porc*, *jambon au sauce Madère* with spinach, *escalope milanaise avec spaghetti*, *mouton chop avec pommes frites* or *cœur de rumpsteak avec pommes rissolées*. Desserts without a supplement are fairly basic, though the *salade de fruits frais* provided a pleasant, light contrast to the strongly flavoured main course. If that doesn't appeal, there's always cheese or *pâtisserie maison*.

Thoumieux   **Map ref: 7E**
79 Rue Saint-Dominique (Mᵒ *Latour-Maubourg*)
Tel: 47.05.49.75
Open: lunch and dinner until 23.30
Closed: Monday
Set menu: 41F
À la carte: 110–130F
Wine: 25F (bottle)
Service: 15%

There are few good, decently-priced restaurants down in the Invalides–Tour Eiffel area, so this is a rare find, and its late hours and Sunday opening are an added bonus. It's got great atmosphere – a 1930s *brasserie*-style interior, with bright lights, potted plants, mirrors, brass rails and traditionally dressed waiters, all combine to give it a style belying its moderate tariff. The cuisine is decidedly south-western, with a strong accent on duck, in which the house specializes, but there's a range to suit all tastes. For the impecunious there's a narrow 41F set menu, offering either *côtes de porc grillées* or omelette as a main dish, but purse permitting we would recommend splashing out à la carte.

For openers there's a surfeit of possibilities – spicy *champignons à la grecque*, a crispy *salade d'épinards aux lardons* (spinach with bacon) and a superb *rillettes de canard* (a coarse duck pâté) all proved winners the night a group of us visited. Inevitably, duck was a major feature for the main dish too – the *cassoulet au confit de canard* was characteristically rich, hearty and copious, and the *filet de canard maison* was a thick, tender steak of duck-breast cooked with loads of garlic and served with sauté potatoes. Perhaps the most adventurous treatment of all was the *cuisse de canard aux pruneaux et filet d'oie fumé* (leg of duck and smoked goose cooked with prunes), which was very popular with the regulars. And rather than stick with the mundane house wine, you couldn't do better, with this kind of food, than the 1981 Cahors Carte Noire – a lovely, inky, mellow, full-bodied red wine.

But there's more to Thoumieux's menu than duck: there are four fish dishes, including *raie au beurre noir* (skate in a butter, lemon, parsley and caper sauce), as well as veal, beef and another favourite, *gigot d'agneau aux flageolets* (lamb with white beans). Only one criticism, common to many restaurants we've sampled, especially those of south-west origin – an unhealthy lack of vegetables with this massive protein fix.

Desserts are perhaps a little run-of-the-mill, with the *pâtisseries* and *profiteroles* being best bets – and we'd definitely advise against the rather tasteless, over-sweet *crème de marrons* (chestnut purée) and those dishes incorporating it, such as *coupe correziènne*. A cheaper, more satisfying and original finale is perhaps the lovely Cabecous cheese, with its chalky edge and distinctive flavour of goat's milk.

Afterwards, if you're down here in the evening, take a post-prandial stroll round the Champ-de-Mars beneath the Tour Eiffel – a picture-postcard stereotype, certainly, but illuminated by night it still has an unforgettable magic.

Le Volant   **Map ref: 15D**

13 Rue Béatrix-Dussane (Mᵒ *Dupleix*)

Tel: 45.75.27.67

Open: lunch and dinner until 22.00

Closed: Saturday lunch, Sunday

Set menu: 72F (until 21.00)

À la carte: 130–140F

Wine: 44F (bottle)

Service: included

In a fairly barren part of the 15ᵉ, just south of the Tour Eiffel, this is not the kind of place you stumble across but is well worth making the trip for. Owned by a septuagenarian former racing driver, Georges Houel, its walls are covered with memorabilia of the sport (by the front door a signed photo of a very young Stirling Moss, which aged us slightly). The dining-room, which spills out onto the pavement in summer, is intimate but not cramped, and both the staff and the youngish clientele are extremely '*sympathique*'. The cuisine is notable for its combination of traditional French elements and a certain lightness of touch – very welcome in the July temperatures in which we visited.

Before 21.00 the restaurant operates an excellent, if short, 72F menu – a delectable, light and creamy *fromage blanc aux herbes*, *terrine de foie de volailles*, *poireaux* (leeks) *vinaigrette* or a palate-freshening *salade aux lardons* for starters. Pick of the main dishes was the *bœuf bourguignon* or the *plat du jour* which was *poitrine de veau* – cold cuts of tender veal, served with cold *haricots verts*, salad and marrow, an ideal and substantial summer salad. À la carte one can steer clear of the usual meat overdose (though as if to underline the French love-affair with the flesh, we witnessed the spectacle of two young women on the next table tucking into enormous slabs of almost raw beef). The Roquefort and walnut salad is highly recommended, as is the *brochette de poisson* – a kebab of small fish steaks served with rice and a mushroom sauce. Other specialities of the house include *escargots*, *rognons de veau grillés au moutarde*, *sole meunière* and a *côte de veau normande*.

Desserts are simple but interesting, and pick of the bunch is a typically French eye-opener, prunes *à l'orange* – forget those wizened bowel-openers covered with congealed custard from school-canteen days; these are lusciously delicate fruits, soaked in red wine and with a tart hint of orange peel. A perfect surprise. With a moderate bottle of wine – we chose a slightly unusual chilled Beaujolais rosé – you could eat very well from the set menu for around 100F, and around 130–150F à la carte.

DELUXE

La Toison d'Or   **Map ref: 15E**
29 Rue Castagnary (Mᵒ *Plaisance*)
Tel: 45.31.52.44
Open: dinner only
Closed: Monday
À la carte: 130–160F
Wine: 35F (bottle)
Service: 15%

This is something very, very special – an exquisite and unusual Russian (Georgian) bistro, established originally by the brothers Antadze and now presided over by a younger offshoot of the family, a sort of vodka-sodden Tony Hancock figure with terrible French and a great sense of style. The interior is done out in timber, like an *isba*, with pewter ikons and piped Russian choirs. It's always packed so a reservation, made several days in advance, is essential – you'll be very lucky to get in on spec.

Toison d'Or is the kind of place where you're set for the evening, so hang loose and let it all happen, helped along with lashings of ice-cold Russian vodka (12F the shot, 115F the bottle). You won't always understand what the waiter is telling you, but the menu is short and even if you go the whole hog you won't break 160F – and with care it could be less. The only expensive item is the wine – there is a house wine at 35F, but for real authenticity the strong, slightly rough Georgian red, at 85F, is an intriguing indulgence.

There are two types of starter – *sougoni grillé* for two, a delicious grilled goat's-cheese dish, and then a range of four separate *hors d'œuvres*, all with their own unique tastes and textures. *Bobio* is a semi-purée of red kidney-beans; the *fromage frais au fines herbes* is like a creamy version of *tsatsiki*; then there's a wonderful *ratatouille* with coriander; and last, but certainly not least, the delicate *caviar d'aubergine* makes up the delectable quartet.

There are only about five main dishes too: most simple are the enormous *brochettes* of pork or lamb, with rice, skewered on deadly-looking swords; lamb gets a more sophisticated treatment in *caourma*, with its tangy orange-red sauce; then there's *takaka*, a ragout of shellfish; and finally *sasivi*, which is chicken cooked and served cold in a walnut sauce. For dessert there's *halva*, *gâteau de fromage* or the amazingly rich *gâteau georgien* (one between two was all we could manage), with its caramel-like filling and lashings of honey and nuts. As we left, the table across the way had just ordered up their second bottle of vodka – it was going to be a long night! It's worth remembering that the Georgians live to 125 on this kind of stuff . . .

THE BEST OF THE REST

Wine-bars – cafés – bars

Sancerre, 22 Avenue Rapp, 7ᵉ (Mᵒ *École-Militaire*) – a moderately-priced wine-bar specializing mainly in interesting Sancerre wines, and also serving omelettes, sandwiches and other light fare.

Au Sauvignon, 80 Rue des Saints-Pères, 7ᵉ (Mᵒ *Sèvres-Babylone*) – a lively, unpretentious wine-bar with unusually late opening hours. A must in November and December, when the Beaujolais Nouveau is flowing.

Salons de thé

La Pagode, 57 bis, Rue de Babylone, 7ᵉ (Mᵒ *Saint François-Xavier*) – in the late nineteenth century some eccentric bourgeois had this pagoda transported from Japan and rebuilt in Paris. Now it's a beautiful cinema, café and tea-room. Delightfully unexpected.

Food-shops

Le Jardin, 100 Rue du Bac, 7ᵉ (Mᵒ *Bac* or *Sèvres-Babylone*) – a rare macrobiotic and vegetarian food-shop and restaurant (untried by us) on one of Paris's classiest streets.

Lionel Poîlane, 49 Boulevard de Grenelle, 15ᵉ (Mᵒ *Bir-Hakeim* or *Grenelle*) – another branch of Lionel's selling France's most famous bread (see also p. 100), this time out on the fringes (relatively speaking) of the 15ᵉ.

Marie-Anne Cantin, 12 Rue du Champ-de-Mars, 7ᵉ
(Mᵒ *École-Militaire*) – a pretty cheese boutique offering 100
well-aged cheeses from all over France.

Max Poîlane, 87 Rue Brancion, 15ᵉ (Mᵒ *Porte de Vanves*) – it's
not well-known that Lionel has a less-famous brother, Max,
who produces a similar line in bread from wood-fired ovens in
this beautiful nineteenth-century *boulangerie*.

Poujauran, 20 Rue Jean-Nicot, 7ᵉ (Mᵒ *Latour-Maubourg*) –
organic bread specialist and *pâtisserie*. Try their *baguette
biologique*, one of the best in Paris.

9e and 10e Arrondissements

Les 'Grands Boulevards' – République –
Gare du Nord

Covering a large section of northern-central Paris, this area
stretches from the chic splendours of the Madeleine and the
Opéra in the west to the ethnic diversity of Belleville in the
east, and takes in two of the city's largest stations and its major
canal. The area is bounded in the south by the '*grands
boulevards*' – one long street which changes its name eight
times en route between the Place de la République and the
Madeleine. Lined for much of its length by street cafés,
restaurant terraces, cinemas and boutiques, for many people it

epitomizes Paris. In recent years it has ceded its stylish popularity to Saint-Germain, Les Halles and Beaubourg, with the result that it has become rather sleazy, particularly along the Poissonnière, Bonne Nouvelle and Saint-Denis. However, just off the boulevards there are some charming reminders of fashionable old Paris, for example the Passage des Panoramas (11 Boulevard Montmartre) and, almost opposite, the Passage Jouffroy.

North of the boulevards lies an anonymous area extending to the next line of boulevards, the even sleazier Clichy and Rochechouart. There's little to remark on here except for the little-known area around Notre-Dame de Lorette – the Rues des Martyrs, Rodier, Milton and the Place Saint-Georges. Dubbed the 'new Athens', it combines a gentle, neo-classical style of building with a village-like atmosphere, and in the nineteenth century was a favourite haunt of the high Romantics – Berlioz, Delacroix, Chopin, George Sand and Dumas.

Down in the south-west corner of the 9ᵉ there's the elaborate, somewhat pompous concoction of Garnier's Opéra, displaying the full range of nineteenth-century neo-classicism – the stairs inside, for example, are truly overwhelming – with a ceiling added later by Chagall. But of course the building was never suitable for its purpose, and in 1989 will cede its place as Paris's principal theatre for opera and ballet to the new building being constructed on the east side of the Place de la Bastille.

Much further east, beyond the two main stations, is one of the city's neglected gems, the Canal Saint-Martin. Once crowded with barge traffic plying between the Seine and the Marne valley to the north-east of Paris, it curves up to the Bassin de Villette at the Place de Stalingrad in the north, and vanishes underground beneath the Boulevard Richard-Lenoir in the south, re-emerging south of the Bastille. Even today, with race-track one-way streets on either side, the Canal Saint-Martin provides a romantic and unexpectedly pleasant promenade, incorporating the Quai de Jemmapes and passing the now run-down Hôtel du Nord, scene of the classic 1930s movie of that name starring Jean Gabin and Arletty.

In culinary terms the area is notable for several old-established, large-scale eating-places, hangovers from the area's more fashionable days. **Chartier** (9A), for example, was appearing in food guides in the 1860s, and prices haven't risen much since! Several of these classic spots are open very late to cater both for travellers arriving at the stations (**Terminus**

Nord, 10C) and for denizens of the thriving night-clubs in this sector of town (**Brasserie Flo**, 10A, **Julien**, 10B, and **Chez Jenny**, 3B, just off the République in the 3ᵉ *arrondissement*). A good area for well-heeled insomniacs.

BUDGET

Chartier   Map Ref: 9A
7 Rue du Faubourg-Montmartre (Mᵒ *Montmartre*)
Tel: 47.70.86.29
Open: lunch and dinner until 21.30 every day

For review and prices see **Le Druout** (2A)

Le Relais Savoyard   Map Ref: 9B
13 Rue Rodier (Mᵒ *Cadet* or *Notre-Dame de Lorette*)
Tel: 45.26.17.48
Open: lunch and dinner
Closed: Sunday
Set menus: 45F, 72F
À la carte: 100–120F
Wine: 35F (bottle)
Service: 15%

Tucked away in a quiet street mid-way between the *grands boulevards* and Pigalle, this reliable, homely Savoie bistro is a good place for either lunch or an evening meal. For starters the 45F set menu offers a choice of *crudités*, *rillettes*, grapefruit, egg mayonnaise, *avocat vinaigrette* (for a small supplement) or an excellent smoked herring with potato salad. For the main course, as well as *steak tartare*, *rumpsteak*, *côtes d'agneau* and *jambonneau* (pork knuckle), there are two light fish dishes: *roussette à la moutard* (a mild, white-flesh dogfish in a tangy mustard sauce), and a more traditional trout with almonds which didn't have the flabby texture and metallic taste of many farmed trout in Britain. Both dishes were served with small waxy, full-flavoured boiled potatoes.

Desserts, too, were equally '*correct*', as the French say: *tarte au pommes* and a fresh *poire au vin*. This mini midday feast, with a bottle of mineral water and service (extra), came to about 60F apiece. In the evening, when you could let loose a little more, the carte offers several regional and house specialities, including *fondue savoyarde* at 50F, *saucisse au vin blanc de Savoie* and an interesting *côte de veau maison flambée* at 52F.

MODERATE

Chez Maurice   Map Ref: 9C
44 Rue Notre-Dame de Lorette (Mᵒ *Saint-Georges*)
Tel: 48.74.44.86
Open: lunch and dinner until 22.30 every day
Set menus: 46F, 67F
À la carte: 90–110F
Wine: 12F (37cl)
Service: 15%
Credit cards: Visa, American Express, Diners' Club

Stuck in an unfashionable limbo between Pigalle and the *grands boulevards*, this is an odd little place with a slightly glitzy, 'modernized' interior, an unexpected penchant for David Bowie music and a tendency towards service à la Fawlty Towers. So don't go if you're in a hurry – it was about fifteen minutes before we even saw the menu. Still, that's its only real drawback. The food is sound, wide-ranging and reasonably cheap, with quite a good fish line-up à la carte: *saumon frais meunière*, *lotte normande*, *lotte au poivre vert* (monkfish with green pepper), trout, sole and *Saint-Jacques provençale*. For lunch, on the cheaper of the set menus, alongside *moules*, *dinde* (turkey hen) *marengo*, *steak grillé* and *andouillette grillée*, we were offered *sole limande meunière* – whole lemon sole freshly cooked in butter and simply served with boiled potatoes. With a *pichet* of very decent white *vin de table*, a substantial herring *hors d'œuvre*, chocolate mousse and coffee to follow, the bill came to a mere 67F.

The slightly more expensive menu offers a wider, more luxurious range of first and main courses, including a fresh salmon or rabbit terrine starter, followed by *escalope à la crème*, *canard au poivre vert* and *côtes d'agneau*. More expensive duck specialities such as *confit de canard* and *magret de canard* are also available.

DELUXE

Brasserie Flo   **Map Ref: 10A**
7 Cour des Petites-Écuries (M° *Château d'Eau*)
Tel: 47.70.13.59
Open: lunch and dinner till 01.30 every day
Set menu: 98F
À la carte: 140–160F
Wine: 28F (50cl)
Service: 15%
Credit cards: Visa

Still one of Paris's classic late-night eating-spots, still providing
excellent food, and still affordable without going into
overdraft. What more to recommend it than that? Its series of
elegant wood-panelled dining-rooms can get very packed with
discriminating eaters, and outside weekday lunchtimes it's
advisable to book. But the inconvenience and the hectic bustle
– all part of its famous atmosphere – are worth putting up with
as you'll never eat badly at Flo.

   Of course it's first and foremost a *brasserie*, and traditionally
that means *choucroute*. If that's your taste, then the *menu
promotionnel* is excellent value at 98F for *hareng de Baltique à
la crème*, *choucroute* with all the sausage and pork trimmings,
sorbet, coffee and half a litre of Riesling. But you may wish to
stray further afield, and Flo has recently introduced some
interesting *nouvelle*-inspired dishes amongst the heavier
classics. For example, after a starter of *cervelas rémoulade*
(sliced garlic sausage with creamy mayonnaise and raw onion
rings), we had the *aiguillette de canard aux fruits*, an intriguing
and colourful combination. The duck was sliced thinly, topped
with a cranberry sauce and accompanied by braised apples and
slices of kiwi-fruit – a successful experiment. Rounding off with
a superb *gâteau glace au caramel* from the extensive dessert-list
– a slice of coffee ice-cream gâteau smothered in caramel and
burnt almonds – the bill came to 150F, including the dry, fruity
house Riesling and service.

   Like all good *brasseries*, Flo is a great place for seafood-
lovers, with its own fresh *coquillage* and *huître* stall on the
street outside. Top of the list, for a real feast, must be the giant
plateau de fruits de mer at 139F, or the grilled lobster *flambé au
whiskey* at the same price. But you don't have to pay all that –
the simple *friture d'équilles sauce tartare* (a large plate of
deep-fried sand eel, like overgrown whitebait) is justly very

popular. Even if you only go once, don't miss a trip to Flo – it's an authentic Parisian eating experience.

Julien   Map Ref: 10B

16 Rue du Faubourg-Saint-Denis (M° *Strasbourg-Saint-Denis*)

Tel: 47.70.12.06

Open: lunch and dinner until 02.00 every day

Set menu: 105F

À la carte: 150–160F

Wine: 61F (litre)

Service: 15%

Credit cards: Visa, American Express, Diners' Club

Another 'classic of the night' just round the corner from **Brasserie Flo** (10A) and even more beautiful. If you want to eat well and in real style, then Julien fits the bill perfectly. A great place for a special treat, it must have one of the most beautiful dining-rooms in the whole of Paris. Step through the doors, on the street-market section of the Faubourg Saint-Denis, just north of the imposing stone arch, and you're immediately transported to the art deco extravagance of the *fin de siècle*. Enormous coloured ceramics and mosaics, extraordinarily florid plasterwork, round, ceiling-high mirrors, stained glass skylights and carved mahogany woodwork all combine to produce the most captivating ambience which one could soak up for hours.

The menu too has its extravagant moments, such as *langoustine froide mayonnaise* at 119F and *langouste grillée et flambé au whiskey* at 149F. But most of the dishes are in the affordable bracket, and very varied. There is a poorly advertised *menu promotionnel* at 105F (look in the small print), but add wine and service and you're going to end up paying around 140F anyway, which is not much less than eating à la carte. Entrées include superb versions of traditional favourites such as *filets de hareng pommes à l'huile* (smoky, tender and served warm) and *frisée aux croûtons et lardons*, topped with a poached egg, as well as *medaillon de lotte à la catalane*, excellent salmon *rillettes*, *terrine de canard*, cold gazpacho and *moules* cooked in Riesling.

Amongst the main dishes there's a heavy beef and lamb bias, but fish can be had in the shape of *suprême de turbot à la graine de moutarde* and *filets de haddock poché à l'anglaise* – smoked haddock in a rich butter sauce with new potatoes. Simple and perfectly presented. For the rest it's such classics as *tête de veau*, *magret de canard*, a renowned *cassoulet* for the winter months, *sauté d'agneau à la fondue de poireaux* and several cuts of beef including *châteaubriant* and *filet de bœuf au Porto*.

And if that's not enough, there's a seductive dessert-list as long as your arm, featuring luscious *profiteroles*, a range of sorbets including the rich, purple-black Cassis version, packed with blackcurrants, and gâteaus galore, such as *succès au citron vert* (a melting lime and coconut concoction) and *gâteau glacé*. Wet the whistle and raise the spirits with a litre of the excellent house Riesling, sit back, relax and enjoy a sumptuous evening. Julien is a rare find indeed.

Au Petit Riche   Map Ref: 9D

25 Rue le Peletier (Mᵒ *Richelieu-Druout* or *Le Peletier*)
Tel: 47.70.68.68
Open: lunch and dinner until 00.15
Closed: Sunday
Set menu: 110F
À la carte: 140–160F
Wine: 25F, 28F (50cl)
Service: included
Credit cards: Visa

An elegant Parisian restaurant of the old school – over 100 years old in this case – of the sort that always looks more expensive and luxurious than it is. Here that impression is conveyed by formally dressed waiters and by the dark wood panels, tall mirrors and starched linen which grace the small, sectioned dining-rooms, where businessmen lunch and a younger, brighter set dine on a mix of traditional and *nouvelle*-inspired cuisine.

Each day sees a new *plat du jour* which comes as the main dish of the 110F *menu promotionnel*: *contrefilet rôti* (Monday), *coquelet à l'estragon* (Tuesday), *gigot d'agneau* (Wednesday), *aile de raie aux capres* (Friday) and *canette de Barbarie à l'orange* (Saturday) was the line-up at the time of writing. Unfortunately Thursday's dish, *bœuf-mode froid aux carottes*, was possibly the least interesting on offer – sliced cold roast beef and carrots pressed in gelatine, served with dressed lettuce. A summer effort which doesn't quite work. The *hors d'œuvre*, *rillettes de haddock*, was superb – a delicate-flavoured coarse haddock pâté beautifully presented in a cream sauce dotted with slices of tomato. And for sweet there's the house speciality, *tarte fine aux pommes chaudes*, which is a refined version of France's favourite dessert – a thin flaky pastry base covered with hot, wafer-thin slices of sweet, browned apples.

The house wines of the Loire – Sauvignon, Gamay or Bourgeuil – served by the carafe, are fine and coupled with the set menu will keep you well within 140F. If the day's specials don't appeal, however, you have a tempting choice à la carte. For example, *jambon persillé de Santenay* or *crottin de chavignol chaud* for starters, and then *darne de saumon poché à la ciboulette, pigeonneau rôti aux légumes tournés* and *pied de porc grillé sauce moutarde.* Not to mention the separate dessert-list or an excellent Brie de Meaux to round off an excellent night's eating in the most charming of surroundings.

Le Roi du Pot-au-Feu   Map Ref: 9E

34 Rue Vignon (Mᵒ *Madeleine*)
Tel: 47.42.37.10
Open: lunch and dinner until 21.00
Closed: Sunday
À la carte: 130–140F
Wine: 50F (bottle)
Service: 15%
Credit cards: Visa

Oh, how we suffered to write this book! This little bistro, as its name suggests, specializes in *pot-au-feu*, the classic winter dish which incorporates boiled beef, bone-marrow and chunky vegetables in a meaty broth. To try it out, we had to wade through this hearty fare at lunchtime in early August, with the temperature hovering around 80 degrees. We survived, and the good news is that while this place may not be the 'king' of the *pot-au-feu* (our experience is limited), and while it is not particularly cheap, it would still make a great eating-spot for the winter visitor.

The place itself is small and intimate, decorated with dolls and old musical instruments. They serve a few standard *hors d'œuvres*, and a handful of other dishes all at 55F: chicken, *côtes d'agneau* and *entrecôte* steak. But obviously their real business is the *pot-au-feu* – an enormous plate of tender beef on the bone, with turnips, carrots, marrow and cabbage, all cooked in a rich broth, accompanied by *cornichons* and Dijon mustard and lots of crunchy bread. House wine in winter is a robust Côtes du Rhône, and in summer a chilled Gamay d'Anjou, both of which go down well. Finish off with the hot *tarte tatin* (apple tart cooked on both sides), topped with fresh, unsweetened cream. If you skip the starter you'll come out around 125F poorer, and many hot, steaming calories richer.

Terminus Nord   **Map Ref: 10C**
23 Rue de Dunkerque (M^o *Gare du Nord*)
Tel: 42.85.05.15
Open: lunch and dinner until 00.30 every day
À la carte: 140–160F
Wine: 50F, 61F (litre)
Service: 15%

There are lots of eating-places around the Gare du Nord, many incorporating '*nord*' in their name, so make sure you get the right one. This one resembles all the others from the outside, but its extensive interior is a beautiful stylistic throw-back to the 1920s: brasswork, acres of plants, period cartoons and posters, plush leather *banquettes*, clusters of light globes, long-aproned waiters and mirrors everywhere, giving the whole place a sense of space and light. The pace gets very hectic, however, so it's not the kind of place for an intimate assignation.

Specialities, as in all *brasseries* with the Alsatian connection, are the *choucroute* dishes served with lashings of sausage, pork and bacon. Another speciality at many of Paris's big *brasseries* is sea-food: crabs, prawns, crayfish and shellfish served up on a bed of ice for 115F a head. Then, Alsatian cuisine being robustly meat-based, there is a range of beef, lamb and steak.

For a light *hors d'œuvre* try the *salade frisée* – curly lettuce served with crunchy fried croutons and pieces of bacon topped with a soft-boiled egg. Other starters are *hareng*, asparagus, smoked salmon, *moules* and *terrine de foie de volailles* (chicken liver pâté). You could follow this with *filet de daurade à la façon mereyeurs*, a very full-flavoured fish cooked in a tomato and mushroom sauce, topped with a subtle *gratinée* and served with boiled spuds. Another possibility is the *merlan frit* (fried whiting). To accompany these lighter dishes, try the house Sylvaner at 26F a half litre if you don't mind your wine a little on the sweet side.

Terminus Nord must have one of the longest dessert lists in Paris: peach or strawberry tart, passion-fruit *délice*, chocolate *charlotte* with vanilla custard, *granité de pommes vertes au vieux Calvados* (apple water-ice with Calvados), *crêpes au Grand-Marnier*, sorbets *à gogo*, and so it goes on. However, the one good thing about *brasseries* is that there's absolutely no compulsion to eat three courses if you don't feel up to it. And we didn't.

The bill for two courses with wine came to 122F, so reckon 150–160F with dessert – a bit high, admittedly, but for a stylish, rather exciting evening out we'd strongly recommend it.

THE BEST OF THE REST

Wine-bars – cafés – bars

Le Petit Château d'Eau, 34 Rue du Château-d'Eau, 10ᵉ (Mᵒ *République*) – a bar-café with a traditional half-moon *zinc* and a pristine, welcoming interior.

Food-shops

Lenôtre, 5 Rue du Havre, 9ᵉ (Mᵒ *Saint-Lazare*) – Paris's king of pastries, Gaston Lenôtre, offers an amazing selection of *pâtisserie*, chocolates, a celebrated *baguette* and a fine selection of regional and decorated breads. He also has shops in the 7ᵉ (44 Rue du Bac), the 16ᵉ (44 Rue d'Auteuil) and the 17ᵉ (121 Avenue de Wagram) *arrondissements*.

À la Mère de Famille, 35 Rue du Faubourg-Montmartre, 9ᵉ (Mᵒ *Le Peletier*) – dating back to 1761, this superb chocolate and sweet shop was recently voted the best in Paris by the readers of *Passion* magazine. It should be good – it's run by a Professor of Chocolate!

11ᵉ and 12ᵉ Arrondissements

Bastille – Charonne – Nation – Gare de Lyon

Running these two *arrondissements* together produces a long segment of eastern Paris running from the Place de la République in the north-east to the Bois de Vincennes in the south-east. Most of the eating-places however are in a much smaller triangle bounded by a literary trio of boulevards – Diderot, Voltaire and Beaumarchais. The greater part of the 12ᵉ has little of interest to offer except the enormous, bizarre Palais Omnisports at Bercy, the tiny cemetery of Picpus where La Fayette is buried, and of course the Bois de Vincennes with its château, zoo, lakes, woods and sports areas. In many ways the equal of the better known Bois de Boulogne, it is certainly a good spot for hot summer days when the city streets get unbearable. At the Place de la Nation there's nothing to attract the visitor beyond the memory of those 1300 heads that rolled beneath the guillotine in just forty-three days during the Reign of Terror.

The 11^e is of greater interest although there's little of substance to visit; it's more a question of atmosphere, street-life and low-key charm. However, it is undoubtedly an area on the up and up, particularly the streets east of the Bastille, which will get their social lift from the arrival of the new opera-house in 1989. Already the Rue de Lappe and the Rue de la Roquette have taken off, with a lively night-time culture of dance-clubs, restaurants, bars and late-night shops. It's a very cosmopolitan area too, the more so the further east you walk – Bretons, north African Jews, Turks, West Indians, Vietnamese and Thais have all made their contribution to the mix of shops and cafés. This intense, multi-ethnic mix can best be appreciated by taking a stroll along the lively and fascinating Boulevards Ménilmontant and Belleville on the eastern boundaries of the 11e, particularly while the street markets are in full swing. (Another lively market, in the 12e, takes place every morning except Monday at the Place d'Aligre, near the Ledru-Rollin métro.)

Towards the Bastille there's a strong indigenous artisanal presence, with numerous small workshops and woodworking factories clustered around the Rue de Charonne and the Rue du Faubourg-Saint-Antoine. Several of our cheaper eating-places exist primarily to provide lunch for these local workers. The Bastille itself is of little interest except for a bronze column marking the site of the old prison symbolically destroyed during the French Revolution. Running south from the Bastille is the pleasantly refurbished marina, the Bassin d'Arsenal, with terraced gardens running down to the locks which take boats into the Seine itself. And just to the south-east there's the Gare de Lyon with its sumptuous and extravagantly decorated restaurant, Le Train Bleu, which is worth calling in to see even if you can't afford to eat there.

Not that the area is short of places where you can afford to eat: partly because of its artisanal and cosmopolitan character, it is particularly strong on cheap lunchtime cafés and moderately-priced restaurants for the evening. And if you want to cut loose on your own, the area round Belleville is good for a whole range of ethnic cuisines. But how long the rest of the 11e will remain a good gastronomic bargain-basement remains to be seen.

BUDGET

L'Artisan   **Map ref: 11A**
9 Rue de Charonne (Mᵒ *Ledru Rollin*)
Tel: 47.00.54.53
Open: lunch and dinner till midnight
Closed: Saturday, Sunday
Set menu: 42F (until 14.30)
Á la carte: 90–110F
Wine: 10F (50cl), 30F (bottle)
Service: included
Credit cards: Access, Visa

When the new Opéra comes to the east side of Bastille in 1989 the whole area will go up market, spelling dramatic changes for restaurants like L'Artisan, only a short Valkyrie-ride round the corner in the Rue de Charonne. No doubt it will make the friendly patron, M. Garcia, a richer man, but it will impoverish the rest of us just a little.

L'Artisan is a clean, bright little place, almost pretty in a homely, *kitsch* sort of way, with its predominantly orange colour-scheme, fringed lampshades, Alpine scenes and floral carpeted walls! And at 42F the set menu (until 14.30 only) is extraordinarily good value. After a nicely peppery *champignons à la grecque*, the *cochon de lait rôti frites* (4F extra) seemed the best choice from the varied menu offering *couscous tunisien au mouton* (the day's special), *rosbif haricots verts*, *blanquette de veau* and *onglet aux échalotes*. And to follow this generous plate of tender pork, a choice of *crème de marron* (a cold purée of chestnut), *mousse au citron*, *Mont Blanc* and *pamplemousse à la crème fraîche*.

There's a fascinating and moderately priced choice of dishes à la carte too (though little fish apart from *truite* and *coquilles Saint-Jacques*) – amongst them several French classics such as *magret de canard*, *escargots*, *fondue bourguignonne* (minimum of two people) and a whole range of beef cuts in various sauces. You'd be hard pressed to go over 100F for three courses with wine; the days of places like L'Artisan are numbered, so catch it while you can before the opera-loving yuppies move in.

Les Cinq Points Cardinaux   Map ref: 11B

7 Passage Saint-Bernard (Mᵒ *Ledru Rollin* or *Charonne*)
Tel: 47.00.89.00
Open: lunch only
Closed: Saturday, Sunday
Set menu: 34F
Wine: 5F (25cl)
Service: 10%

Here's an obscure and unusual place to head for if you're down near the Bastille at lunchtime. Situated in a most unlikely street of run-down and abandoned artisans' workshops, it is a bustling working-class diner which hasn't forgotten its history or that of the neighbourhood: around the walls hang many tools of the old trades of the quarter – planes, saws, chisels, hammers – as well as naive, Légeresque paintings and murals. Little more than an extended bar, with a kitchen open to view at the back, the menu offers about five choices of starter and various *plats du jour*. The starters include such staples as egg mayonnaise, pickled herring, tomato salad and pâté, while the main courses get a little more interesting – the day we were there, *lapin coquillettes* (rabbit with macaroni), *viande froide salade* and *morue parmentier salade* (salted cod with potato salad) seemed sound bets, and portions were very generous. Then to finish there's the choice of either the cheese-board or sweets such as chocolate éclair and lemon tart.

Nothing sophisticated here, but for an authentic working-class atmosphere, a bit of hidden history and a cheap, filling lunch, this curio is just the place.

La Ravigote   Map ref: 11C

41 Rue de Montreuil (Mᵒ *Faidherbe-Chaligny*)
Tel: 43.72.96.22
Open: lunch (Monday to Saturday) and dinner until 21.30
        (Thursday to Saturday only)
Closed: Sunday
Set menu: 60F, wine and service included
À la carte: 100–120F, service included
Wine: 24F (50cl), 44F (bottle)

One of a number of delightful, lesser-known eating places in the 11ᵉ, this is a little gem that's great for either lunch or an early evening meal and where the cheap set menu belies the quality of the food. In a tall cool room plastered with romantic old photos of Paris, slightly abstract sports paintings and a sculpture made from kitchen utensils, you can enjoy an excellent range of dishes, with wine and service, for a mere 60F. Summer entrées included an excellent *crudités* served with pieces of cold fish, *foie de morue avec citron*, *poireaux à la vinaigrette* and *terrine de foies de volailles au poivre vert*. For a main dish you could choose *tête de veau*, *truite meunière*, *bavette d'aloyau* (sirloin of beef) *aux échalotes* or the *veau froid* – beautiful tender pieces of veal in a cream sauce, served with rice and a small salad. Then finish off with the excellent *clafouti* (in the cherry season) or the creamy *fromage blanc*. Great cuisine at the lowest prices.

À la carte you can sample a range of excellent fish dishes, including *coquilles Saint-Jacques*, *escalope de saumon à l'aneth* and *sole belle meunière*, alongside such classics as *cassolette de cagouilles*, *cassoulet* and *ris de veau*. Wine and a more expensive dessert could take you up to the 120F mark, but even so you wouldn't regret it.

MODERATE

À Canoa   Map ref: 11D
131 Rue Oberkampf (Mᵒ *Ménilmontant*)
Tel: 43.57.15.47
Open: dinner only until midnight
Closed: Sunday
Set menu: 70F, two courses
Wine: 35F (bottle)
Service: 15%

If **Dona Flor** (2D) in the town centre is a bit expensive for you, here's a wonderful budget-priced Brazilian restaurant really worth travelling for – and a good place for eating in a group. The welcome and service are great, the atmosphere popular and animated, and the food first-class. The chef is Brazilian, but the other staff are truly cosmopolitan – as if to prove that Paris really is the melting pot of Europe, our waiter (a really '*sympa*' guy, as the French say) had a Polish-Jewish mother and Tunisian Berber father!

The menu is simple: for 70F you get a tangy lemon and white wine aperitif, plus two courses (no starter, and you honestly don't need one). There are only five main dishes, headed by the classic *feijoada*, the Brazilian *cassoulet* – spicy pork sausage in a black bean sauce, served with a rice salad and the ever-present bowl of manioc. There are interesting fish dishes too, such as *peixada*, a fish-steak cooked in a spicy coconut sauce, with red peppers, and *camarões mocorongo* (prawns in a maize and coconut sauce). Intriguing combinations, which are matched by the only chicken dish, *xinxin de galinha* – shredded chicken cooked with peanuts. All these should be accompanied by copious amounts of wine – a French house wine is available, but for a slightly light-hearted treat there is the semi-sparkling Portuguese Vinho Verde, or a more sombre, round, full-bodied 1979 Torres Sangre de Toro from Spain, which is perfect with the *feijoada*.

But leave room for the desserts – although there are only three, they're all extraordinary: *torta de banane* (banana tart with cinnamon), *bolo de chocolat* (a chocolate ice-cream gâteau with lemon) and *torta frai de abacaxi* (a pineapple sorbet). Wonderful ways to end a fascinating and inexpensive meal, which won't cost you more than 115F, no matter how hard you try.

Anjou-Normandie   **Map ref: 11E**
13 Rue de la Folie-Méricourt (Mᵒ *Saint-Ambroise*)
Tel: 47.00.30.59
Open: lunch and dinner until 21.30
Closed: Saturday, Sunday, Monday dinner
Set menus: 77F, 86F, service included
À la carte: 120–130F, service at 15%
Wine: 30F (bottle)
Credit cards: Visa (for sums over 200F)

Not far from the République and within walking distance of Père Lachaise cemetery, Anjou-Normandie's cool, calm interior is worlds away from the Boulevard race-tracks of the 11ᵉ. Ideal for either lunch or dinner, it is important to remember though that there are two distinct à la carte menus, one for lunchtime and one in the evening, though the 77F and 86F set menus (the latter looking very good value) apply throughout the day.

The food here is lighter than its south-western counterparts (with little evidence of the dairy overdose normally associated with Normandy cuisine), and the menu proudly announces that no artificial colourings are used. The service by not-so-pretty boys in rather ridiculous *paysan* smocks is willing but not over-efficient. Starters include copious *crudités*, *moules en cassolette* (shelled mussels in a butter, parsley and garlic sauce served up in its own little pot), pâtés, *œuf mayonnaise* and *avocat*. For the main lunch course we chose *filet d'élingus* – a breaded hake-like fish served in a piquant mustard sauce – and *pintade farcie* (guinea-fowl with a superb pork and sage stuffing), tomatoes and sauté potatoes. We accompanied this with a 50cl *pichet* of the crisp, clean house Muscadet.

The food so far had been good, but the desserts topped it. The menu cryptically states that the availability of puddings 'depends on the mood of the chef', so obviously he'd had a good day. We chose two different sponge gâteaus: one with apricots and almonds, *'flottant'* in a lake of creamy custard, the other on dry land with a raspberry and cream filling. *Mmm*!

This rather extravagant lunch came to 81F each, including coffee and service. In the evening, on the 86F menu (service included, drinks extra), you might push that up to around 100–120F at most. Specialities of the house include three types of their much vaunted *andouillettes* (sausages) – 'the best in Paris' – and a very reasonably priced *magret de canard* at 59F. All in all well worth the trip.

Café Melrose's   Map ref: 12A

76 Avenue Ledru-Rollin (Mᵒ *Ledru Rollin*)
Tel: 46.28.10.82
Open: lunch and dinner until 23.00
Closed: Sunday lunch, Monday
Set menus: 50F (lunch only), 69F, 89F, service included
À la carte: not recommended
Wine: from 42F (bottle)

The gay scene in Paris is visibly thriving, compared with several years ago, and this friendly little restaurant in the 12ᵉ, with its predominantly gay clientele and staff, is just one spin-off. Straights seem very welcome too, judging from our visit. The exterior is unprepossessing, but a minute frontage conceals an unexpectedly roomy, comfortable interior with tiled floors, fringed lampshades and contemporary abstract watercolours on the walls. There are two set menus, 69F (50F at lunchtimes only) and 89F, which we'd recommend in preference to eating à la carte as that could run up much more expensively.

The set menus, particularly the dearer one, are quite varied. Entrées offer some interesting salads – *salade campagnarde* and *salade auvergnate* both incorporate ham and cheese and nuts, while the *frisée aux lardons* has bags of hot, crispy bacon. The *crottin de Chavignol grillé* is highly recommended – grilled goat's cheese on toast, with a *frisée* side salad, sprinkled with pine-kernels. Main dishes range from the usual varieties of meat – *onglet aux l'échalotes*, *brochette de bœuf*, *ris de veau*, all served with *pommes sautées* – to a short fish list which includes *truite* and *haddock meunière*, beautifully prepared in a butter sauce with new potatoes, and an excellent *darne de saumon grillé béarnaise* (grilled salmon in a Béarnaise sauce). Portions are only average but the standard of cuisine is well up to scratch. However, service can get rather erratic, not to say distracted, as the place fills up after 21.00.

Finishing off with one of their interesting desserts, such as *délice Melrose's* (a slice of thick chocolate mousse-cake in a *crème anglaise*), an above average *île flottante* or the lip-staining, lip-smacking *sorbet Cassis*, plus half a bottle of wine, and you'll come out under 120F, or 100F on the cheaper menu, or even less at lunch.

Chez Adé   **Map ref: 12B**

35 Rue Traversière (Mᵒ *Gare de Lyon*)
Tel: 43.07.27.70
Open: dinner only until 22.30
Closed: Sunday, Monday
À la carte: 80–90F
Wine: 21F (litre)
Service: 15%

Another little eating-place, this time down near the Gare de Lyon, where *antillais* cuisine once again come up trumps. It is a simple, unpretentious, family-run place with a TV by the bar (running a dubbed version of *The Thorn Birds* to a small, attentive audience when we were there), and the food is plentiful, cheap and delicious. Though the menu is short, it contains the best-known *Antillais* staples: *court bouillon de poisson*, *poulet* or *porc au curry* and *poisson frite antillais* – red kidney-beans and rice must be ordered separately. You write your own order – a tradition in many *antillais* restaurants, apparently – and depending on the number of customers and the popularity of the TV programme, service is prompt and attentive.

Starters include *morue* (cod) or *crevettes* (shrimp) *accras*, *boudin antillais* or a simpler plate of *crudités*, and the house wine is cheap and cheerful, though a heartier Côtes du Rhône or an excellent, fruity Beaujolais Villages, at little extra cost, make the food go with an added zing. Finish off with a coconut or exotic fruit-based dessert – *sorbet au fruit de la passion*, lychees, *glace coco* or *ananas flambé*, for example – and you'll have sampled an excellent range of basic Antillean cuisine, with wine, for between 80F and 90F.

Jacques Mélac   **Map ref: 11F**
42 Rue Léon-Frot (Mᵒ *Charonne*)
Tel: 43.70.59.27
Open: 08.30–19.00 (midnight on Tuesday and Thursday)
Closed: Sunday, Monday

This is not strictly a restaurant, but Jacques Mélac's tiny wine-bar, not far from the Bastille, is such a wonderful institution that it's worth considering for a more liquid night out. In fact it's a must for wine-lovers, and you can also eat there: generous plates of *charcuterie*, a range of Auvergne cheeses, substantial omelettes and a special hot dish every day, all accompanied by the wonderful crunchy, fragrant *pain poîlane*. But the food is intended only as an accompaniment to the wonderful range of reasonably-priced wines assembled by Jacques Mélac himself. (Other drinks are definitely frowned upon: a notice on the wall announces that 'water is strictly for boiling potatoes'!)

Jacques, a young, likeable Auvergnat with a handle-bar moustache, will discourse with you for hours in incomprehensible French about the respective merits of the fifty lines he turns over. On the right of the bar the bottles are simply displayed with their take-away prices, while 'drink-in' prices (roughly double), appear on a blackboard behind the bar. The wine is still good value, with several bottles in the 40–60F range. It is best to go in a large group, if possible, so that you can sample several wines, though many can be bought by the glass. On the night we were there, six of us managed to sample (in the pursuit of our profession, of course) six different wines, including a flowery Beaujolais Villages, and a less illustrious but equally light and fruity cousin from the same grape, Gamay de Touraine. Then there was a superb Saint-Joseph, a meaty, brick-built wine from the Rhône which overshadows anything of that name sold elsewhere. Also recommended is the Saumur Champigny, an unusual red wine from the Loire, made from the Cabernet Franc grape, which has bags of character. And if you've never had it before, finish the evening with a glass of the luscious Muscat de Beaumes de Venise – a superbly rich, luxurious dessert-wine from the Rhône smelling of all the fruits you've ever tasted, and more besides.

A warning note: Mélac's place can get addictive, not to say blurred, and on good nights closing times are entirely notional provided you're already in there. We were still cheerfully supping our last drops of Muscat at 1.30 a.m. And it does get very, very full, though in summer tables spill out onto the street. For good wine, good company and a cheerful atmosphere, this place is a must.

L'Occitanie   Map ref: 11G

96 Rue Oberkampf (Mᵒ *Saint-Maur* or *Ménilmontant*)
Tel: 48.06.46.98
Open: lunch and dinner until 22.30
Closed: Saturday lunch, Sunday
Set menus: 39F, 72F
À la carte: 80–100F
Wine: 14F (50cl), 25F (bottle)
Service: 15%

L'Occitanie was the old kingdom of the South before the unification of France, and amazingly there is still a minority who keep alive the old language and culture, and campaign for regional autonomy. The tradition is maintained in this fascinating and cheap little restaurant, not too far from the République, in its bilingual menus ('*toupi del jorn*' – *plats du jour*; '*rafres quit*' – *crudités*) and in a cuisine which diverges distinctly, though subtly, from run-of-the-mill traditional south-western cuisine. Interesting elements of Basque, Spanish and Italian cooking are legacies of a culture that spread right across the south of France.

There are two set menus, at 39F and 72F, the cheaper of which is very good value; but if you want to sample some of the specialities, you are advised to go à la carte, which with wine should not run to more than 100F. For starters there is an interesting range of omelettes, including *omelette quercynoise*, with Roquefort cheese and walnuts; a tempting range of large, crispy, well-topped pizzas such as the *royale occitanne*; and delicious salads such as *salade cevenole*, with rice, lettuce and chestnuts.

Main courses too are intriguingly different: a *poulet gratinée*, topped with ham and cheese and a tomato sauce and served with rice; *rôti de lapin farci* (stuffed, roast rabbit); and a lentil dish, *salcissa de tolosa*. Other Occitaine favourites are the *cassoulet de mas* (farmhouse *cassoulet*); *aubergine al formatjade* (an aubergine and cheese dish) and *pavé aux baies de groseilles* (steak cooked with red currants) – all interesting enough to warrant more than one visit.

The desserts don't let you down either: several are based on figs, such as fig sorbet in a fig liqueur and *tarte aux figues*, and there's also *pêché mignon*, which is mint ice-cream in a hot chocolate sauce – *mmm*! All in all a unique establishment, where you can tap into the deepest roots of French history.

DELUXE

La Galoche d'Aurillac   **Map ref: 11H**
41 Rue de Lappe (Mᵒ *Bastille*)
Tel: 47.00.77.15
Open: lunch and dinner until 22.30
Closed: Sunday, Monday
À la carte: 120–140F
Wine: 30F (bottle)
Service: 15%

Situated in an amazing little street near the Bastille, among a mix of up-and-coming clubs and bars and decaying, picturesque artisanal premises (including the former workshops of the company which made the old zinc counters for Paris's countless bars), this place can best be described, in culinary terms at least, as *heavy*: Auvergne cuisine is amongst the richest and most meat-based in the whole of France, so don't come here expecting a light lunch. (Vegetarians and semi-veggies, steer clear.)

The atmosphere and décor match the food perfectly: traditional, sombre, varnished woodwork everywhere, the ceiling covered with wooden clogs, and a low, old-style bar-counter running half the length of the room. Sadly the host and his staff suffer from a distinct lack of front-of-house PR – the waitress in particular was possibly the sourest and least helpful in the entire city – but the food is first-class, though winter is undoubtedly the time to appreciate it at its best.

Entrées are varied and copious. An enormous *salade du Cantal* incorporates lettuce, Cantal cheese and pieces of ham. The *pâtés d'Auvergne* offers three enormous slabs of pâté, including a fascinating stuffing-like variety, moulded around whole plums! And if those don't appeal there are *escargots*, *soupe au fromage avec crème fraîche* (cheese soup with cream) and *ballotine de lièvre* (boned, stuffed hare). Everything accompanied by the crusty, brown *pain de campagne*.

Main courses, with the exception of the succulent, gamy *confit de canard*, served with sliced potatoes sautéd in duck fat, are meat, meat, meat all the way. No fish or poultry graced the menu on our visit, though from time to time a superb *lapin à la moutarde* appears as dish of the day. Normally it's such regional specialities as *onglet de bœuf*, *bavette d'aloyau* (sirloin) *garnie*, *tripoux du Cantal* or *saucisse d'Auvergne aux lentilles*. Red wine is a must, either the house *pichet* (from a bottle of that name, confusingly) or the heavy, almost inky-black Cahors, which complements this robust fare perfectly.

Desserts here are highly recommended, among them *soufflé glacé au Grand-Marnier*, a sort of half-way house between cheese-cake and ice-cream, *tarte au myrtille*, *tarte aux fraises* and *charlotte chocolat poire*. All served with a small bowl of *crème fraîche*. For three whole courses, with wine, you can reckon on paying around 120–140F each, but you'll certainly know you've eaten. Good food; shame about the staff.

THE BEST OF THE REST

Wine-bars – cafés – bars

Le Baron Rouge, 1 Rue Théophile-Roussel, 12ᵉ (Mᵒ *Ledru Rollin*) – a combination of wine-shop and a tiny bar at the back where you can taste before you buy. Take your own bottles and they'll fill them from barrels from 8F a litre.

Le Carrefour, 116 Rue Ledru-Rollin, 11ᵉ (Mᵒ *Ledru Rollin*) – a pleasant, bright, art nouveau style bar in a lively part of the 11ᵉ.

Le Clown Bar, 114 Rue Amelot, 11ᵉ (Mᵒ *Filles du Calvaire*) – a crazy old neighbourhood dive full of nostalgic mementos of the

Cirque d'Hiver which is housed almost next door. 'Closed due to the heat,' last time we visited, 'but will open when the monsoon comes.'

Le Savoyard, 39 Rue Popincourt, 11ᵉ (Mᵒ *Saint-Ambroise*) – a wonderful old-fashioned *épicerie* selling cheeses, wines and meat, with a bar for taking the odd drink, almost in the Irish style.

Food-shops

Aux Cinq Continents, 75 Rue de la Roquette, 11ᵉ (Mᵒ *Voltaire*) – a lovely shop selling a wide range of wholefoods – nuts, cereals, etc. – in bulk.

Sarrazin, 120 Rue du Faubourg-Saint-Antoine, 11ᵉ (Mᵒ *Ledru Rollin*) – a wonderful *pâtisserie* and chocolate-shop. Great fruit tarts.

Vong-Linh, 19 Rue de la Roquette, 11ᵉ (Mᵒ *Bastille*) – a very ordinary-looking shop recently voted 'best friendly grocer' by *Passion* magazine. A grocer and Laotian deli combined, open till 23.00. Try their delicious homemade '*pâte impérial*' egg-roll.

13ᵉ Arrondissement

Les Gobelins – Place d'Italie – Butte-aux-Cailles

Throughout the eighteenth and nineteenth centuries the 13ᵉ
arrondissement had a distinctive, almost autonomous character
of its own, and a remarkable degree of well-respected infamy.
In the period between the two revolutions of 1789 and 1848 it
was the home of the poorest and most rebellious sections of the
Parisian population – in 1848 and during the Commune of 1871
the people of the 13ᵉ were always first on the barricades. In the
nineteenth century many small factories and workshops were
established there, in particular a substantial tanning industry
drawing on the waters of the River Bièvre which used to
meander through the area towards the Seine. Despite – or
because of – the extremely crowded and insanitary living-
conditions of the quarter, the worker-inhabitants soon created
a thriving social and cultural life of their own on the streets and
on the boulevards; so poor was this area, in fact, that the eating
of horse-meat was institutionalized here, in the form of Paris's
first horse-butcher who set up shop in 1866. And Victor Hugo

situated several episodes of *Les Misérables* in Les Gobelins.
Up until the Second World War the whole area, with its cafés,
bars and cinemas, possessed a popular cultural identity
renowned all over the city. After the war, however, this now
somewhat anonymous sector of the city went through a
wholesale transformation: the factories moved out, large areas
were destroyed and rebuilt, rents went up and most of the
working population were rehoused in the suburbs or in the ugly
high-rise concrete apartment-blocks which mar the whole
south-eastern skyline. The more pleasant parts of the
arrondissement, on the northern fringes around the Boulevards
Arago and Saint-Marcel, are now inhabited by well-heeled
professionals who contribute little to the cultural and social
ambience of the area.

Although there are no monuments of note here, and
although much of its social and architectural fabric has been
destroyed, there are one or two pockets of this older Paris –
diminishing windows onto the past – worth looking up. One of
them is the area known as Butte-aux-Cailles ('*la Butte*'), a
warren of older streets north of the Rue Tolbiac and east of the
Avenue d'Italie (one of our restaurant choices, **Le Ménestrel**,
13B, is located here), whose inhabitants jealously defend the
distinct 'village' atmosphere that still survives against the odds.

But not all the changes to the 13ᵉ have been negative. In
recent years there has been a large influx of Asiatic immigrants
– Laotians, Vietnamese, Cambodians, Chinese – forming a
heterogeneous community which now constitutes about ten
per cent of the population of the *arrondissement*, with the
Chinese in the majority. And of course the gastronomic culture
has profited enormously, with over 100 south-east Asian
restaurants in six square kilometres. These are concentrated in
three main areas – Boulevard Massena/Avenue de Choisy, the
Rue Baudricourt and the Rue Dunois/Boulevard Vincent-
Auriol. While we have included only two of the most
celebrated here, readers really shouldn't be afraid of cutting
loose on their own and sampling others – the generally low
prices guarantee that individual exploration certainly won't be
a costly exercise.

BUDGET

La Nouvelle Gare   **Map Ref: 13A**

49 Boulevard Vincent-Auriol (Mᵒ *Chevaleret*)

Tel: 45.84.74.29

Open: 24 hours

Closed: Sunday

Set menu: 38F

À la carte: 60–70F

Wine: 16–18F (litre)

Service: 12%

Here's one for the not-so-well-off insomniac abroad. While there are several restaurants in Paris which open round the clock (see Index), they do tend to be chic and expensive. This one isn't, though admittedly it's not very central either. Located in a fairly industrial area by the Seine in the south-east, La Nouvelle Gare is a long-standing working-class institution, providing sound, traditional cooking in enormous quantities at knock-down prices. Fronted by a seedy bar, it has no décor to speak of and no other concessions to style, and the main entertainment is provided by an over-friendly cat which forces it seductive attentions on the nearest approachable diner.

However, the food is excellent at the price, and with a menu as long as the night itself there's amazing variety on offer – for example, nine pâtés on the entrée list and ten different cheeses to finish. Main courses are legion, with seven fish dishes, four styles of rabbit and voluminous cuts of beef and lamb, alongside classics such as *canettes aux olives*, *pot-au-feu*, *bœuf bourguignon* and *coq au vin* – and none at more than 40F the dish, most at much less. And whatever you choose, there's always a small mountain of *frites*, boiled potatoes or pasta so you won't go away hungry. Desserts are boringly basic, and after the gargantuan first two courses probably superfluous.

You won't eat the most sophisticated cuisine in the world here, but as you stagger away into the night or day, you'll feel a little heavier and your wallet only a little lighter.

Le Ménestrel   **Map Ref: 13B**

10 Rue de l'Espérance (Mᵒ *Corvisart*)

Tel: 45.89.14.08

Open: lunch and dinner until 23.00

Closed: Saturday, Sunday lunch

Set menu: 54F

À la carte: 110–130F

Wine: 25F (bottle)

Service: 15%

Hiding behind an ordinary-looking bar-front in a working-class district, this bright, pine-tabled place is a nice surprise, offering a wide-ranging and inventive cuisine at reasonable prices. The 54F set menu is particularly good value: amongst a choice of starters, which include tarama, *charcuterie* and *frisée aux lardons*, the simplest dish, *crudités*, is recommended as one of the best versions of this *hors d'œuvre*, in range, presentation and freshness, that we have sampled.

The main course, *escalope de volaille normande*, was a delightful surprise – large slices of tender turkey in a subtle lemon sauce, with an enormous plate of freshly cooked *frites*. Other possibilities included *filet d'aiglefin à l'indienne*, *palette rôtie à la diable* and *bavette à la bordelaise*, all bringing slightly more culinary flair than usual to a menu at this price.

The carte offers more exciting surprises – entrées such as *crottin de Chavignol* (a firm goat's cheese) *flambé au Cognac*, *gazpacho andalou* and *les oeufs brouillés à la monégasque* (eggs Monaco), then some tempting fish dishes which include *escalope de saumon à l'oseille*, *filet de lotte poêlé au beurre ou poivre vert* (monkfish fried in butter or with green peppercorns) and *la bourride spéciale de la maison* (a fish and shellfish soup made with eggs and served with *aïoli*). If you want to be really extravagant, the *assiette norvégienne* offers a huge plate of salmon, herring, caviare, smoked haddock and taramasalata, accompanied by a glass of ice-cold vodka.

Perhaps only the desserts are a touch disappointing, and off the set menu could be easily overlooked – the *mousse au chocolat* was only middling in the great French mousse-of-the-year stakes, and the *pâtisseries* and sorbets looked ordinary. The house-wine, *en pichet*, is fair – in our case a half-litre of crisp, chilled Sauvignon, though bottles start at 25F. On the set menu, depending on your capacity for drink, you could eat well for around 70–80F with wine and service and even à la carte you'd be hard-pushed to top 125F for cuisine with a lighter touch and some distinctive moments.

Le Palais de Cristal   **Map Ref: 13C**

70 Rue Baudricourt (Mᵒ *Tolbiac*)
Tel: 45.84.81.56
Open: lunch and dinner until 22.00
Closed: Wednesday
Set menu: 45F
À la carte: 70–80F, two courses
Wine: 33–35F (bottle)
Service: included
Credit cards: Visa

One of the few good things about the emigration of the
middle-class Vietnamese under French colonial rule and then
during and after the Vietnam War is the addition of their
cuisine to the Parisian culinary scene. Paris has many
Vietnamese eateries, a few of them chic and expensive, most of
them occupying the cheaper ground. The cuisine itself, while
similar to Chinese food, has a certain delicacy for palates used
to Cantonese dishes liberally laced with monosodium
glutamate.

  Le Palais de Cristal is far from offering the most
sophisticated variants of south-east Asian dishes, but for sound
quality and sheer quantity the 45F set menu here is one of the
best deals in town. But don't go expecting a leisurely, romantic
evocation of the Mekong Delta – this place is modern,
businesslike and bustling with Vietnamese workers (always a
good sign). You could eat à la carte with wine from the shortish
menu for around 80–90F, but the set menu makes sense even
though you don't get to choose your dishes. Strangely, you get
the best value by eating alone: a beef and cabbage soup, two
main dishes such as *assiette de riz au bœuf sauté aux légumes*
and *riz de poulet à la vapeur* (between two people you get a
selection of only three dishes), an enormous bowl of rice, as
much tea as you can drink, and a small sweet rice-and-bean
concoction for dessert. The hot soup and main dishes arrive at
the same time, to be eaten alongside each other.

  As well as the simple range of basic dishes, with vegetables in
a slightly spicy sauce (*riz au poulet*, *gambas*, *porc* or *bœuf*)
there's a range of specialities including some enormous, filling
bowls of soups and noodles, such as *vermicelli de riz au bœuf* at
26F, which are as good as a full meal. All in all the Palais de
Cristal is an excellent place for a cheap, substantial lunch,
though to sample the full range of Vietnamese cuisine you'd
have to eat elsewhere, and slightly more expensively.

MODERATE

Etchegorry   **Map Ref: 13D**
41 Rue Croulebarbe (Mᵒ *Corvisart* or *Les Gobelins*)
Tel: 43.31.63.05
Open: lunch and dinner until 22.30
Closed: Saturday lunch, Sunday
Set menu: 60F, 102F, service included
À la carte: not recommended
Wine: from 50F (bottle)

The laudable French institution of the *menu promotionnel* or *menu conseillé* is one of the best ways of eating cheaply and well in Paris, and here's a good example of its advantages – a fairly high-class, well-appointed restaurant where eating à la carte would probably take you well out of our price range. Yet the two set menus, at 60F and 102F (wine extra), enable one to sample three of the cheaper and mid-priced dishes quite inexpensively.

Etchegorry, despite its oriental-sounding name, is actually a Basque-Béarnaise restaurant, located in a quiet street not far from the Place d'Italie. It has a slightly quaint, *faux-rustique* interior, all flowered wallpaper, brassware, red velvet curtains and oil portraits of mysterious historical personages, yet the ambience is certainly not unpleasant. Features of the two set menus are the excellent *piperade* (a hot semi-purée of tomatoes, eggs, peppers and cheese, topped by pieces of bacon), the *soupe de poisson* and the *salade de confits*, which is vegetables pickled in vinegar or alcohol. A perennial favourite is *poulet fricassé basquaise* – chicken topped with a rich tomato and pepper sauce, served with rice – while seafood-lovers can luxuriate in *chipirons à l'encre* (squid in its own ink) or *paella* (for two people only). And of course duck and pork figure strongly too – *porc confit et pommes à l'huile* and *confit de canard*.

For dessert the most authentic item is the *gâteau basque*, an apparently simple sponge, all moist, rich and seductively sweet. Those with an even sweeter tooth should try the *tranche au Cassis* – a perfumed red-purple Cassis sorbet, served in enormous quantities. Wine is not cheap, at around 50F the bottle, but even so on the cheaper menu you can eat for around 100F, and on the dearer one, about 130F. The service is excellent.

Fortune des Mers   **Map Ref: 13E**
55 Boulevard d'Italie (Mᵒ *Tolbiac*)
Tel: 45.85.76.83
Open: lunch and dinner until 23.00
Closed: Sunday, Monday
Set menu: 45F, 80F, two courses
À la carte: from 140F
Wine: from 36F (bottle)
Service: 15%

Probably the biggest and certainly the most recently opened restaurant in Paris devoted entirely to fish. Very modern, very stylish, with lots of greenery festooning its glitzy, split-level interior, it's actually a three-in-one place, with prices ranging from the affordable to the astronomic. Most expensively there's the 'Hommard Bleu' section which, as its name suggests, is the province of the lobster and the up-market end of the marine range; the mid-priced 'L'Araphoes' seems to occupy most of the two floors; and then upstairs you can sit at the bar of the 'Lady Jane' for the 45F set menu or anything else you fancy. Service is slow, even at the bar, though the young, predominantly gay waiters compensate with a certain amount of friendly charm.

But what of the food? The 45F 'American Cup' (don't ask us why) set menu is limited but substantial: to start, a *panaché de poissons crus* (three types of raw fish); then *filet de maquereaux sauce mousseline* accompanied with a purée of carrot, beans, ratatouille and salad); and to finish, half an Ogen melon. Very refreshing. There's also an 80F '*plateau corvette*', for which you get a selected entrée and a main dish. After that the other set menus skyrocket to 200F. Wine is on the dear side (especially when they've 'run out' of the cheapest white, Gros Plants de Nantes) – a bottle of Muscadet is 42F.

If you're feeling slightly more flush and expansive, the sea-bottom is the limit here. The *fruits de mer* list includes all the expected delicacies – *langoustines*, *huîtres* (oysters) and *oursins* (the spiny sea-urchin, cut open and eaten raw – a French delicacy we have yet to get our minds around). There's also *sole du Croisic au beurre fondu citronnée* (sole cooked in lemon butter), *escalope de saumon sauvage à la nantaise* (salmon with a cream sauce) and *bar de ligne grillé aux herbes* (grilled sea-bass with herbs). Nor do they skimp on the desserts, with a range of *charlottes*, an enormous *opéra de sorbets* (many flavours, many colours) and a more simple *tarte du jour*.

Unless you have the basic set menu you won't eat cheaply here, but for good, well-prepared, well-presented seafood, Fortune des Mers are the specialists.

Thuy Huoung   **Map Ref: 13F**
15 Avenue de Choisy (M° *Porte de Choisy*)
Tel: 45.86.87.07
Open: lunch and dinner until 22.00
Closed: Thursday
À la carte: 70–90F
Wine: from 35F (bottle)
Service: included

After twenty-five years as a restaurateur in Phnom-Penh, Mr Liao Yaou and his family got out in 1974, happily just before Pol Pot arrived. For ten years now he's been running this great little Cambodian-Vietnamese restaurant (his wife is from Vietnam) down in the deep 13ᵉ at the Porte de Choisy. The setting, amongst a bustling cluster of other Chinese and south-east Asian eating-places in a modern mall (le Kiosque de Choisy), overlooked by massive tower-blocks, is not pretty, but don't be put off – for interesting food, a friendly welcome and superb value for money. Thuy Huoung's fame extends far beyond this out-of-the-way enclave.

Service is relaxed and friendly, and even though the place is always busy Mr Yaou will come round and chat to you about the food and anything else that takes his fancy. The menu is quite a varied one. You could start with their *soupe namya speciale* (fish and coconut), or the highly celebrated *dun thang* – a *bouillon de vermicelles*, *pâté de porc*, *crevettes sechées* and chicken. Then there's the *crêpe cambodgienne Thuy Huoung*, a crispy omelette of beansprouts, pork and vegetables; *brochettes* of pork or beef; or the *ravioli special Thuy Huoung*. Whatever you choose, you won't go wrong.

Then, unusually for a south-east Asian restaurant, there's a great dessert-list, with various *délices* and sweet *compotes* of rice, nuts and fruits which are like exquisitely flavoured creamy mini rice puddings. At the end of all this, replete and completely charmed, you won't have spent more than 80–90F each for a soup, two dishes, rice, a dessert and half a bottle of wine. Cambodia's loss was certainly Paris's gain.

THE BEST OF THE REST

Wine-bars – cafés – bars

Le Merle Moqueur, 11 Rue de la Butte-aux-Cailles, 13ᵉ
(Mᵒ *Corvisart*) – a popular café with jazz and folk music.

Food-shops

J. C. Vanderstichel, 31 Boulevard Arago, 13ᵉ (Mᵒ *Gobelins*) – a
great, straightforward bread-shop specializing in organic
loaves such as the *baguette biologique*.

Tang, 48 Avenue d'Ivry, and *Paris-Store*, 44 Avenue d'Ivry,
13ᵉ (Mᵒ *Porte d'Ivry*) – two magic south-east Asian
supermarkets, selling a wide range of exotic foods such as
glazed duck and a wide variety of rices and fruits.

14ᵉ Arrondissement

Montparnasse – Denfert-Rochereau – Plaisance – Pernety

Forming a huge triangle on the Left Bank, the 14ᵉ is most famous for Montparnasse on its northern edge, the epitome of artistic café society in the early part of this century. The Boulevards Montparnasse and Raspail are still amongst Paris's most chic places to drink and be seen, even if they have been literally overshadowed by the distinctly un-artistic Tour Montparnasse (see the 15ᵉ *Arrondissement*, p. 101).

But the 14ᵉ is much more than a posing-ground for the rich and cultured. For a start, the dead make almost as much impact as the living in the fascinating Cimietière Montparnasse, last resting-place of a host of luminaries such as Baudelaire, Brancusi, Zadkine, Tzara, Soutine, Proudhon, Saint-Saëns and de Maupassant. More recently there's Jean-Paul Sartre and Simone de Beauvoir, who after their inspiring years of struggle and commitment now lie together in the cemetery's plainest grave. And don't miss the bizarre tomb of a certain M. Pigeon (against the wall in Sector 17) who commissioned the life-size sculpture of himself in bed with his wife as his mortal testament!

South of the heart of Montparnasse lies the appealing area of Plaisance–Pernety, around the Métro stations of the same names. A distinct village which was only absorbed by Paris in the nineteenth century, it remained a densely-packed mix of workers and artists, with a lively local culture, up until the 1950s. But as with the 13ᵉ, the property boom years after the war wrecked this socially cohesive community. In the Seventies urban planners devised a scheme to drive an autoroute south from Montparnasse to the Périphérique, via the Rue Vercingetorix, which would have displaced 2000 families in the process, but the project was successfully defeated through a broadly-based local campaign. Although this and subsequent actions have slowed down the decay of the area, the population of the 14ᵉ has declined over twenty per cent in twenty-five years, and most of the old factories have closed down or moved out. As you'll see from our restaurant choices, the influx of migrants – in this case Afro-Caribbeans – has done most to reinvigorate the area, but the absence of any eateries in our Budget category reflects the lack of a local working-class community and the growing market value of property within reach of Montparnasse.

The best glimpse of the former splendour of the old village of Plaisance is to be found amongst the remarkable villas around the Rue d'Alésia – the Villa Jamot and others off the Rue Didot, for example, or the Villa Léone off the Rue Bardinet, which have beautiful elongated courtyards of greenery and peace, cut off from the bustle of the twentieth-century city. There are similar clusters of these squares and tranquil cul-de-sacs further east, below the Avenue Denfert-Rochereau, the most beautiful being the Villa Adrienne, off the Avenue du Général-Leclerc.

Further south on the outer fringes of Paris proper, just north of the enormous Cité Universitaire complex, is one of the city's least-known parks, the Parc Montsouris, where Lenin is known to have taken regular constitutionals while living near by in the Rue Beaunier. Another creation of Baron Haussmann (though designed by Alphand) to match the Parc des Buttes Chaumont in the north-east of Paris, it has its own oriental folly and artificial lake.

The Bars of Montparnasse

Vying with the cluster of famous cafés in Saint-Germain (see the 6ᶜ *Arrondissement*, p. 89) are three celebrated haunts on the Boulevard du Montparnasse, all equally expensive. But again, if you can't resist the lure of the illustrious artistic and intellectual past, here's a run-down on their long-gone clientele and the current state of play:

La Coupole, 102 Boulevard du Montparnasse (Mᵒ *Vavin*). Something of a late-comer (it opened in 1927), it has a vast art-deco railway-station feel to it and serves mediocre, over-priced meals till 01.00. Downstairs there is a dance-hall. Always popular with Americans since its grand opening – Dos Passos, Henry Miller, Hemingway and Man Ray frequently passed through its doors – it is still the place to see and be seen.

La Rotonde, 105 Boulevard du Montparnasse (Mᵒ *Vavin*). A remodelled, rather charmless version of the place Lenin and Trotsky frequented, while debating revolutionary tactics before the First World War, and where Louis Aragon picked a fight with the proprietor in 1923.

La Closerie de Lilas, 171 Boulevard du Montparnasse (Mᵒ *Vavin* or *Port-Royal*). Of all these Montparnasse bars, this has probably maintained its charm the most, with its superb décor, large polished tables, oak and copper-covered bar and mosaic floor. Dating back to the nineteenth century, it was the regular meeting-place of several generations of artists – Verlaine, Baudelaire and Mallarmé, and then Henry James and Hemingway. The names of other regular *habitués* are even inscribed on the tables – Max Jacob, André Breton, Modigliani, Strindberg and Lenin.

MODERATE

La Bergamote   **Map ref: 14A**

1 Rue Niepce (Mᵒ *Pernety*)

Tel: 43.22.79.47

Open: lunch and dinner until 22.30

Closed: Sunday, Monday

Set menus: 50F, 70F, 80F

Wine: from 46F (bottle)

Service: 15%

Credit cards: Visa, American Express

Why is it that many of the best Parisian eating-places are tucked away in the most unprepossessing back-streets? This one, in a run-down, unfashionable part of Montparnasse, looks like a Stoke Newington café, with marble-topped tables, tiled floor and a whirring overhead fan, but the overall effect is of a cool and relaxed atmosphere in which to sample some unexpectedly excellent food.

The restaurant is owned and run by a young couple, clearly under the influence of *nouvelle cuisine*. But they've turned its conventions to their own purposes, to create dishes with real flair at reasonable prices and in good-sized portions. The menu is short and varies daily according to season – your guarantee that the food is freshly prepared with good quality ingredients. There are three '*formules*', including a lunchtime '*Rapide*' (50F) consisting of an entrée and a *plat du jour* (*rognons aux épices* on the day we visited). The 70F *formule* offers an entrée, a choice of five hot dishes, and a dessert; and the 80F evening menu throws in a salad and cheese.

Entrées are unusual and imaginative – an orange salad marinaded in a curry sauce, an aubergine caviar and a smoked salmon mousse. Main dishes come gently spiced in their own sauces, often with unusual vegetables such as puréed beetroot or braised celery: veal in coriander, lamb with thyme, and a *panaché* of fish including *rascasse*, *lotte* and cod.

Desserts are prepared with the same imaginative flair – a rhubarb *clafouti*, *pruneaux aux épices*, a variety of sorbets and one of the best *marquise au chocolat* in town. A delicious ending to an almost perfect meal.

La Créole   Map ref: 14B

122 Boulevard du Montparnasse (Mº *Vavin* or *Port-Royal*)

Tel: 43.20.62.12

Open: lunch and dinner until 22.30 (23.00 on Saturday and
Sunday)

Closed: Sunday lunch

Set menu: 60F

À la carte: 140–160F

Wine: from 45F (bottle)

Service: 15%

Credit cards: Visa, American Express, Diners' Club

Down in chic Montparnasse, looking far more expensive than
it is, this new Martinique restaurant is an astounding find.
Although they lost our reservation, and we had to wait fifteen
minutes for a table, from that inauspicious beginning
everything else looked up: we got a cocktail on the house to
make up for delay – '*Le Planteur*' (passion-fruit juice, white
rum and ice in a glass with a sugared rim, one of several
exotically intoxicating mixes on offer). And the meal was
certainly worth the wait.

The first startling thing about La Créole is the décor – an
absolute riot of Caribbean motifs, all done with considerable
flair. If there's such a thing as *kitsch* with style then this is it,
particularly the rear dining-room where the greenery is
densest. Huge plastic palms prop up the ceiling, baskets dangle
down, plastic flowers and fruit jostle with enormous prints on
the walls, small spotlights pick out pools of colour, calypso
throbs out at low volume – and the pace is hectic, with packed
tables and a quicksilver staff darting about with dishes of
wonderful looking food. Even before you've tasted a morsel,
you're hooked on the experience.

When the food comes you know you're on to something
special. Even on the 60F set menu (possibly the best value in
Paris) the food is exquisite. Go à la carte, probably for a
maximum of 150F with wine, and you're in a tropical culinary
paradise. We started with *accras*, which are deep-fried, herby,
spicy balls of airy dough, with lettuce (a small caveat – the
boudin créole, a small blood sausage, is an acquired taste). This
was followed by *colombo de porc* – deliciously tender pieces of
pork in a light curry sauce served, like everything here, with a
bowl of fluffy rice and gently spiced kidney-beans, which are
very substantial. *Tarte coco* followed, a delectable tart made with
shredded coconut, baked to a golden brown on top and melting

away in the mouth – one of the best treatments of coconut we've tasted. Accompanying the meal with a half bottle of refreshingly chilled Anjou rosé (popular with Antilles cuisine) and a coffee, we paid only an amazing 93F each.

Other Caribbean delights on the menu here include *crabe farci* (stuffed crab) and avocado with crab and shrimps for starters. Crab also features as a main dish in the house *tour de force*, *matoutou*, an enormous, whole stuffed crab, served with side salad and lashings of fried rice. Other highly recommended fish dishes include *blaff* (fish cooked with onions in a spicy sauce) and *court bouillon*, while meat-eaters could delight in *steak antillais*, *poulet fricassé* and *columbo de poulet* (treated much the same as the pork, above). And whatever you choose here, the service and presentation are exceptional – let's just hope that success doesn't go to their heads, as more and more Parisians discover that their former colony is now running French cuisine very close on style and flavour.

Le Flamboyant   Map ref: 14C
11 Rue Boyer-Barret (M° *Pernety*)
Tel: 45.41.00.22
Open: lunch and dinner until 23.30
Closed: Sunday dinner, Monday, Tuesday lunch
Set menu: 41F (lunch only)
À la carte: 90–110F
Wine: 10F (50cl)
Service: included

Just as some of the best eating-places in Britain are the ethnic ones with a colonial connection, so too in France, though the colonies and cuisines are in most cases entirely different. One small part of the French empire was the Antilles Islands (Guadeloupe and Martinique), at the southern end of the Caribbean, and tucked away in this unfashionable, working-class district of Paris (not far south of Montparnasse Cemetery) is a restaurant where you can sample this interesting cuisine at its best.

The *antillais* taste and style is quite different from anything we've experienced in Britain, even in West Indian cooking of the Jamaican variety. It's based essentially on sea-food and fruit, light in texture but strong on pepper and spice. Le Flamboyant is bright and lively, with heavily Caribbean décor, and is presided over by a genial, welcoming proprietor. Service is brisk but friendly even at the height of a Friday night rush.

Starters include *accras*, *gambas vinaigrette*, *boudin créole* and an excellent Caribbean salad incorporating carrots, lettuce, peppers and palm kernels, with a tasty, peppery dressing. Then it's further into the unknown, with *aubergines gratinées* in coconut milk, the popular stuffed crab and a range of poultry and fish dishes. These include *poisson du Flamboyant* (served cold), a superb *poisson frit*, and *blaff*, a flavourful if somewhat bony variety of fish cooked with onions in a delightful spicy sauce. All dishes come with filling bowls of white rice and red beans. It seems that rosé is the most popular wine with such fare, though cold lager would be just as appropriate.

Desserts too are no ordinary line-up: at around 25F there's a range of rum- and liqueur-laced ice-cream *coupes*, incorporating coconut, mango, passion-fruit, etc., as well as the same sort of thing minus the booze. And there's an enormous chunk of fresh pineapple to clean the palate. One black mark though: the Caribbean fruit salad contained at least some tinned fruit and the whole thing was over-loaded with sugary syrup. Considering that they were selling fresh exotic fruits at a greengrocer only a few doors away, this was unforgivable. Otherwise this place is well worth a trip south for an eating experience you couldn't get in Britain, though you should always book first or you could be disappointed.

N'Zadette M'Foua   Map ref: 14D

152 Rue du Château (Mᵒ *Pernety* or *Gaîté*)
Tel: 43.22.00.16
Open: dinner only
Closed: Sunday
Set menu: 48F
À la carte: 110–125F
Wine: 20F (50cl)
Service: 15%

We'd heard some good reports of this unique Congolese restaurant situated down a side street off the Avenue du Maine. In its tiny dining-room they try hard to re-create a bit of the Congo with exotic wooden carvings, stuffed snakes and the rhythmic sound of Burundi drumming over the PA. A young and appreciative clientele, palates no doubt jaded by eating French bourgeois cuisine '*en famille*', flock to the restaurant each weekend, smoking themselves and you to death in the process.

Normally we have no hesitation about urging adventurousness when it comes to the menu in most restaurants, but here we sound a note of caution: stick with our recommendations unless you already know a lot about African cuisine. For starters, we recommend *sourire congolais*, a coconut bowl brimming with cucumber, pineapple and prawns in a thick, creamy sauce on a bed of lettuce; or the *brochette brazzavilloise*, a kebab of beef, Congolese style. Next opt for the house speciality, *moukalou au M'Foumboua*, a delicious and unusual concoction of smoked haddock in a rich peanut sauce. Vegetables are extra and not over-ample – choose from plantains, potatoes, manioc, etc., at approximately 10F a portion. The desserts are all fresh fruit, and the house wine is more than drinkable.

You can either eat à la carte as we did or opt for the set menu at 48F which is probably a good introduction to this kind of food. Frankly, we thought the food a little disappointing, and much blander than we'd expected. But if you're tiring of French cooking and want to try Congolese food for yourself, then this is a reasonable place to come.

DELUXE

Le Cerf-Volant Créole   Map ref: 14E
58 Rue Daguerre (M° *Denfert-Rochereau* or *Gaîté*)
Tel: 43.20.21.59
Open: lunch and dinner until 23.00
Closed: Sunday, Monday lunch
À la Carte: 120–140F
Wine: 20F (50cl)
Service: 15%
Credit cards: Visa

There are three restaurants in a row on this street serving *réunionnais* cuisine (from the tiny South Indian Ocean island of Réunion), and this one is the most popular and stylish with its all-white, colonial-style façade and interior. (See also **L'Isle Bourbon**, 18C). Reservations are a must, but well worth the trouble.

Réunionnais cuisine is a unique blend of elements from both Afro-Caribbean and Indian traditions, with local style thrown in. For entrées there are such things as *avocat au crabe* (avocado stuffed with crab and onion, in a cream sauce), *rougail de morue* (cold fish with a spicy, highly perfumed purée of tomato, pepper and onion), and *langue de bœuf au gingembre* (beef-tongue in ginger). *Rougails* or *caris* (curries) make up the bulk of the main courses – *cari de poisson* and *cari de volaille* are lightly curried fish and chicken dishes, while the *rougail de crevettes* is a strongly flavoured purée of (dried?) shrimps with the unique *rougail* sauce, accompanied by kidney-beans and rice (ordered separately here).

A good all-in deal is the '*Assiette créole*' which offers you choice of a main dish with rice and a side-salad for 53F. A chilled *pichet* of house rosé slips down nicely with this style of food, and to finish, desserts are sumptuous concoctions of fruit, ice-cream and Chantilly. Treat yourself to a '*Coupe des Îles*' (vanilla, coconut, exotic fruits, rum and Chantilly) or 'Coco Nut' (vanilla, coconut, chocolate, banana and Chantilly). Dining à la carte, with the pick of the menu plus wine, expect to pay around 130F.

La Route du Château   Map ref: 14F
36 Rue Raymond-Losserand (Mᵒ *Gaîté* or *Pernety*)
Tel: 43.20.09.59
Open: lunch and dinner until 02.00
Closed: Sunday, Monday lunch
Set menu: 65F
À la carte: 130–160F
Wine: from 35F (bottle)
Service: 15%

This is a pretty and relaxed little restaurant tucked away in a part of the 14ᵉ just starting to gentrify. In fact it has most things going for it – varied, inventive cuisine, pleasant atmosphere and service, reasonable prices and late opening hours. So for those driven away from the Boulevard du Montparnasse by the exorbitant hype and streets full of poseurs, it's an excellent refuge.

The 65F menu is a real winner. For openers there's a choice of *terrine de campagne*, *poireaux à la vinaigrette* (leeks in a vinegar dressing), *saucisson d'ail* (garlic sausage) or the *museau à la rémoulade* (chopped muzzle of veal with a French dressing). Main dishes are even more intriguing, and include *gratin de quenelles de brochet* (pike dumplings on a skewer with a cheese sauce) and the superb *lapin sauté au cidre* (rabbit in a cider and mustard sauce, accompanied by a separate dish of *courgettes gratinées* – an irresistible combination). To finish, the *gâteau glacé* and the *far aux pruneaux* (a flan packed with sweet tender prunes) are the most interesting items.

There are several specialities to be recommended from the *carte* too, such as *gratin de cabillaud* (cod), *canette rôtie* (roast duck), *noix de veau aux girolles* (nuggets of veal cooked with wild mushrooms) and a justly-famed *coquelet au Bleu d'Auvergne* (chicken cooked in the Auvergne's version of Roquefort cheese), served in enormous quantities with sauté potatoes and a vegetable purée. Wines are not cheap, but with a moderate bottle of Bordeaux rosé or Côtes du Rhône, an exceptional culinary indulgence in pleasant surroundings can be yours for around 150F.

THE BEST OF THE REST

Wine-bars – cafés – bars

Le Père Tranquille, 30 Avenue du Maine (Mᵒ *Montparnasse*) – a misnamed wine-bar with erratic opening times and run by a notoriously irritable owner. (Sounds great, eh? You have been warned.) Good wines and open sandwiches.

Le Rallye, 6 Rue Daguerre (Mᵒ *Denfert-Rochereau*) – a plain little workers' wine-bar on the pedestrian market section of the Rue Daguerre.

Le Rosebud, 11 bis Rue Delambre (Mᵒ *Vavin*) – a long-established Left Bank bar frequented by the bohemian and artistic fringes. Stays open until 02.00.

Ty Jos, 32 Rue Delambre (Mᵒ *Vavin*, *Edgar Quinet* or *Montparnasse*) – a simple, Breton-owned bar-café, next to a restaurant of the same name (untried by us). Specializes in Breton folk music.

17ᵉ and 18ᵉ Arrondissements

Montmartre – Barbès – Pigalle – Wagram – Ternes

We've rather arbitrarily lumped these two *arrondissements* together for convenience, but in fact they have very little in common. The 18ᵉ contains at its centre two of the touristic honey-pots of Paris: Montmartre, with its much painted Place du Tertre, stomping-ground of the likes of Picasso, Matisse, Utrillo and Braque before they 'emigrated' to Montparnasse after the First World War; and on the summit of '*la butte*' the imposing Basilica of Sacré-Cœur, built by the Catholic Church to atone for the massacre of 20,000 Communards in 1871. Regardless of its dubious history, and the present-day tourist hordes, it is a must for the view of Paris you get from the church steps – or even better from the dome itself (237 bracing steps) – which is spectacular by day or by night (though the dozens of visitors you see at night hoping to take a photo of the city with a flash-camera are going to be mighty disappointed when they get home!).

But despite the perpetual invasion, Montmartre, away from

the Place du Tertre, has preserved a lot of its authentic character. This is a result partly of its discouraging location (the *butte* of Montmartre is very steep and is riddled with old mine-workings which make new construction risky) and partly of a persistent community spirit, personified in a philanthropic local society which calls itself '*la République de Montmartre*'. A wander round the upper slopes of the *butte* – the Avenue Junot and the Rues Saint-Vincent, des Saules (with the famous cabaret, Le Lapin Agile) and Chevalier-de-la-Barre – reveals a host of delightful old buildings, cobbled streets, picturesque steps and unexpected curios. Amazingly, right behind Sacré-Cœur, in the Rue Saint-Vincent, is one of Paris's few remaining vineyards, a remnant of an illustrious winemaking past, which turns out 500 bottles of red Clos Montmartre each year. More sobering, further west there's the rambling, shady Cimetière de Montmartre, running Père Lachaise and Montparnasse close for illustrious corpses – de Vigny, Stendhal, Berlioz, Degas, Dumas *fils* and more recently François Truffaut amongst them.

The eastern side of the 18ᵉ – the Rue Barbès, the Place Château-Rouge and the Rue de la Goutte-d'Or – is now a densely-settled, heterogeneous immigrant area, occupied initially by Algerians (the Rue de la Goutte-d'Or was a stronghold of the FLN in Paris during the Algerian War), but followed more recently by Antilleans and Africans. The accent here in our choice of eating-places is heavily ethnic, but since we can only scratch the surface, as in the south-east Asian areas of the 13ᵉ, readers are recommended to experiment. Premium prices and unstinting quantity generally make eating-places in this area a very good bet.

By contrast the 17ᵉ is something of a cultural and culinary wasteland. In fact we make no restaurant recommendations here at all – just some interesting shops and bars in our 'Best of the Rest' listing. It could be described as a slightly less expensive extension of the 8ᵉ and 16ᵉ, with wide, featureless boulevards, *fin-de-siècle* apartment-blocks and a noticeable lack of street-life, though there are one or two corners worth catching sight of – for example, the great street market of the Rue de Lévis and the charming Square des Batignolles with its neighbouring church of Sainte-Marie, tucked away behind the railway goods-yards. And a small, unexpected piece of countryside awaits you in the Cité des Fleurs, between the Avenue de Clichy and the Rue de la Jonquière – a peaceful alley of gardens and trees. But apart from these few glimmers amongst the grey, the 17ᵉ needn't detain you long.

BUDGET

Hariti (Andrieu)   **Map ref: 18A**
52 Rue de la Goutte-d'Or (Mᵒ *Barbès-Rochechouart*)
Tel: 42.64.99.16
Open: lunch and dinner until 22.00
Closed: Tuesday
À la carte: 50–80F
Wine: 20F (bottle)
Service: 15%

If the money's a little low, or you're just tired of French cuisine
and want a change, do what you might do in Britain – go ethnic,
in this case Algerian. The 18ᵉ and 19ᵉ *arrondissements* abound
with cheap *couscous* restaurants, but this is undoubtedly one of
the best. Just a short stroll down the hill east of Montmartre
and Sacré-Cœur, it lies just off the Barbès, in the run-down
Rue de la Goutte-d'Or (where Zola set much of *L'Assommoir*,
incidentally) behind a frontage which deceptively advertises
the 'Restaurant Andrieu'. It looks fairly uninspiring from the
outside, but remember you're not here for the décor.

Hariti carries a full menu of French dishes, but to have them
would be like having steak and chips down at the local Indian.
They offer a range of *hors d'œuvres* such as anchovies, tuna,
sardines, palm hearts and pâté. We started with an excellent
tomato salad but wouldn't have bothered if we'd known what
was to follow, in the shape of the *couscous royal* (36F) (they
also serve mutton *couscous* at 28F, *merguez*, a spicy sausage, at
27F, and beef at 27F). First off you are brought a small Saharan
dune of extremely fine-grained *couscous*; then a bowl of spicy
sauce, laced with beans, carrots and courgettes; and finally an
enormous platter of mixed meats, including a quarter chicken,
two *merguez* sausages and about half a pound of lamb and beef.
Although much of this would turn a vegetarian stomach, the
vegetable sauce and *couscous* alone would make a very
acceptable non-meat dish.

We washed this lot down with a bottle of the house red (20F),
although they also stock a wide range of Algerian wines whose
robust character goes well with this hearty national dish. The
whole delicious and filling ensemble came to 68F each,
including service which was polite and friendly, though you
could stoke up here for less than 60F. And that's good value.

MODERATE

Chez Aida   Map ref: 18B
48 Rue Polenceau (Mᵒ *Château Rouge* or *Barbès-*
    Rochechouart)
Tel: 42.58.26.20
Open: lunch and dinner until 23.00
Closed: Wednesday
À la carte: 80–100F, two courses
Wine: 40F (bottle)
Service: included

Around Barbès there's a wide range of ethnic eating-places to
explore, from Bulgarian to Brazilian. This place is one of the
best-known African restaurants, serving the best of Senegalese
food in enormous quantities. The dining-room is bright, clean
and relaxed, with a discreet show of African carvings and a
good range of Afro-Caribbean music on the juke-box. Service
is laid-back and somewhat chaotic – in fact they got our order
completely wrong – but the copious and interesting food itself is
the saving grace.

The menu is short and simple (for a Senegalese at least) with
about eight starters and the same number of main dishes.
Entrées include *salade tomate*, *salade crevettes*, *avocat crevette*
and a wonderful (and cheap) *crabe farci* – shredded crab with a
spicy tomato and pepper dressing and its own small side-salad.
Certainly one of the best first courses we've had in Paris. A tip,
though: unless you're ravenous, ignore the entrées.

For the main course we ordered *mechoui*, a rich African
lamb-stew incorporating half the animal and served with
enough rice for three. But when after twenty minutes a *poisson
braisé* arrived instead, we settled for that. This enormous
tureen of braised fish cooked with cabbage was equally fine, but
compared with the other dishes a little expensive. Other
specialities are the *maffe* (a chicken stew cooked with
vegetables, peanut butter and chillies, *bourakhe* (a beef and
spinach dish) and more simple *brochettes* of meat. Any one of
them will feed you for a day.

L'Isle Bourbon   Map ref: 18C

8 Rue Eugène-Sue (M° *Marcadet-Poissonniers*)

Tel: 42.55.61.64

Open: lunch and dinner until 22.00

Closed: Monday

À la carte: 70–80F

Wine: 7F (50cl), 28F (bottle)

Service: 15%

Credit cards: Visa

Here's a restaurant serving a cuisine we never knew existed
before we first sampled it. A geography lesson – where's
Réunion Island? Answer: in the South Indian Ocean, between
Madagascar and Mauritius. This superb little restaurant on the
north side of the hill at Montmartre specializes in food from
that far-flung outpost of French colonialism, and great food it is
too, combining elements of West Indian and Asian cuisine in a
unique style and at bargain prices.

There are two main themes in *réunionnais* cuisine –
rougailles (or *rougails*) and *cari*. The former is a hot spicy purée
of tomatoes, onions and crushed green peppers (strength and
hotness to order, here), with a perfumed undertone in some
versions. We started with *rougailles de sardines*, a sharp and
tasty opener which can also be combined with ginger, pistachio
or mango chutney. Other likely entrées include *soupe
de homard* (lobster soup), *salade d'avocats* and *avocat farci*.
Then it's on to the *cari* (curry), derived from its sister curries
only two thousand miles away to the north-east. These
réunionnais caris are quite mild and spicy and come in several
varieties, including *poisson*, *crevettes*, *volaille* and *agneau*.
Rice is the obvious main accompaniment, but alternatives (or
supplements) include *haricots rouges*, lentils and the *fricassé de
brèdes* (very close to the Indian *sag bhaji*, but consisting of
spinach, onions and lots of garlic). The popular drink here,
either alongside or instead of wine, is cardamom tea by the
pichet, either hot or cold according to season.

Desserts are not a strong suit, though there are one or two
coconut-based sweets such as the *bombon coco* (a pink, sweet
slice of desiccated crystallized coconut) and the usual lychees,
guavas and passion-fruit (but be prepared for a tinned variety).
For all this you'll pay no more than 75F, which for cuisine of
this standard and uniqueness, is extraordinarily good value.

DELUXE

Marie-Louise **Map ref: 18D**
52 Rue Championnet (Mᵒ *Simplon*)
Tel: 46.06.86.55
Open: lunch and dinner until 21.30
Closed: Sunday, Monday
Set menu: 80F
À la carte: 140–150F
Wine: from 45F (bottle)
Service: 15%
Credit cards: Visa

The furthest north we stray in this book, only one stop from the end of the Métro line, this mini-Mecca of French traditional bourgeois cuisine beyond the *butte* of Montmartre is well worth the trip. Its small, intimate rooms on two floors, with pristine white tablecloths, heavy cutlery and gleaming brassware, regularly attract a loyal, slightly ageing but food-loving clientele. The food is classic fare, with few surprises, but everything perfectly executed and presented. For example, the *frisée aux lardons* is packed with hot, crispy bacon and large *croûtons*, the lettuce is choice and the vinaigrette dressing just so. Similarly the *salade maison*, a finely chopped *mélange* of celery, lettuce, ham and mushroom, in a light mayonnaise sauce. Anchovies and herrings too are prime, full of flavour and of ample proportions.

The main course list is not extensive, but includes a range of fish, meat and poultry – *lotte au pâtes fraîches au basilic* consists of flavoursome pieces of fried monkfish with fresh pasta in a tomato and basil sauce, while the *poularde Marie Louise* is fatted hen in a cream and paprika sauce with rice. Then there's the famous *coq au vin*, *filet grillé sauce béarnaise*, *turbot beurre fondu* and *rognons de veau au Madère* (veal kidneys in Madeira). Wines are on the dear side but there's a sound Muscadet at 45F and an interesting Alsace Pinot Noir (rosé) at 54F which would complement all but the heavier meat-based offerings.

To finish there's an excellent *crème caramel* (reputedly the best in town), an enormous chocolate mousse or an unbeatable *clafouti*. À la carte, reckon around 140–150F; on the set menu, with a more restricted line-up, about 125F. And we bet you can't stagger to the top of Montmartre afterwards (we couldn't).

La Pomponette

Map ref: 18E

42 Rue Lepic (Mᵒ *Blanche* or *Abbesses*)

Tel: 46.06.08.36

Open: lunch and dinner until 22.00

Closed: Sunday dinner, Monday

À la carte: 140–160F

Wine: from 39F (bottle)

Service: 15%

At the top end of one of northern Paris's most lively street-markets and food-shopping streets, just where the Rue Lepic takes a U-shaped diversion, this place is what eating in Paris is all about – unpretentious décor and atmosphere, friendly, middle-aged waiters, creative but largely traditional cuisine and enormous quantities of food. Just the place for a group Saturday lunch, spreading way into the afternoon, or a special evening meal followed by a stroll up to Montmartre or round Pigalle.

The first thing you notice is the unexpectedly airy feel to the L-shaped dining-room behind the bar, with its central servery and walls covered by old prints and paintings. The second is some of the delicious fare – copious salads and gâteaus – on the refrigerated display-table to the left. One of the treats on show is Pomponette's star entrée, a superb *maquereau au vin blanc*, which sets up the meal a treat. Other possibilities are *escargots*, herrings or the mountain of deliciously fresh *crudités*.

The main course choice is doubly difficult, with the long, printed menu supplemented by a series of specials on a weekly rota, some of which tend towards the *nouvelle* – a recent innovation which some think slightly out of character. However, the *suprème de turbot à la moutarde*, served with chopped courgette, was stylish enough. More orthodox perhaps are the excellent *confit de canard*, *tête de veau* (enormous slices of tongue and brain) and another favourite, *noisettes d'agneau basilic*. Poultry too is very well-handled: the *magret de canard* is served two ways, either with green peppers or in a subtle, slightly tart lemon and orange sauce; and the perfectly roasted *cailles* (quails) are topped with cherries which complement them wonderfully.

Desserts too pack quite a culinary punch, front-runners being the famed *profiteroles* and the *charlotte au fromage blanc*, awash in raspberry sauce. With a bottle of moderately priced wine – we shared a Muscadet and a Provence rosé between five – the whole affair will run out top whack around

160F. Not the cheapest meal you'll eat in Paris, but for some, possibly the most memorable.

THE BEST OF THE REST

Wine-bars – cafés – bars

L'Épicerie de la Butte, 11 Rue du Mont-Cenis, 18ᵉ (Mᵒ *Jules Joffrin*) – just ten yards from the Place du Tertre, one of the most tolerable and least spoiled bistro-bars in the area.

Lux Bar, 12 Rue Lepic, 18ᵉ (Mᵒ *Blanche*) – a lovely bar in the middle of a great street market, with a superb ceramic mural of the Moulin Rouge dating from 1910.

Aux Négociants, 27 Rue Lambert, 18ᵉ (Mᵒ *Château Rouge*) – a lovely little wine-bar not far from Sacré-Cœur, with an old semi-circular bar. A good range of wines for 4–6F a small glass, and two or three hot dishes at lunch.

Le Pain et Vin, 1 Rue d'Armaille, 17ᵉ (Mᵒ *Ternes*) – just down the hill north from the Arc de Triomphe, this wine-bar serves wine from 42F a bottle, plus a wide range of sandwiches and *salades* from 25F.

Food-shops

Alain Dubois, 80 Rue de Tocqueville, 17ᵉ (Mᵒ *Villiers*) – a dedicated cheese-shop which supplies a dozen of Paris's best restaurants. Specialists in goat's cheeses.

Boutique du Pain, 11 Rue Gustave-Flaubert, 17ᵉ (Mᵒ *Ternes*) – named after the owner, Monsieur Pain, as well as the product, a bread-shop with a great *baguette de campagne* and *baguette biologique*.

Bromeneau, 59 bis, Rue du Mont-Cenis, 18ᵉ (Mᵒ *Jules Joffrin*) – a very health-orientated *boulangerie* specializing in macrobiotic and biologically pure bread.

Fromagerie de Montmartre, 9 Rue du Poteau, 18ᵉ (Mᵒ *Joffrin*) – a wonderfully pretty cheese-shop ideal for window-shopping or sampling cheeses fresh from the farm.

Jean Carmes et Fils, 24 Rue de Lévis, 17ᵉ (Mᵒ *Villiers*) – another great cheese-shop situated in the street market of the Rue de Lévis, one of the few popular parts of the 17ᵉ.

Lenôtre, 121 Avenue Wagram, 17ᵉ (Mᵒ *Ternes* or *Wagram*) – another branch of one of the city's most renowned *pâtisseries* and *chocolatiers* (see also p. 123).

Le Moule à Gâteau, 10 Rue Poncelet, 17ᵉ (Mᵒ*Ternes*) – another branch of this scrumptious cake and tart shop (see also p. 86).

Pâtisserie Montmartre, 81 Rue du Mont-Cenis, 18ᵉ (Mᵒ *Jules Joffrin*) – an all-round maker and vendor of superb quality cakes, tarts, chocolates, *brioches* and ice-creams. Cholesterol-ville *extraordinaire*.

Pâtisserie Viennoise, 11 Rue Poncelet, 17ᵉ (Mᵒ *Ternes*) – this street is thick with cakes of the Austrian variety, which means apple strudels, spiced cookies and *engadines* (with walnuts) amongst other things.

19ᵉ and 20ᵉ Arrondissements

Père Lachaise – Belleville – Ménilmontant –
Buttes Chaumont – La Villette

On the north and east fringes of the city lie two little-known
arrondissements which contain some of the most fascinating
communities and interesting features. Both are long-
established working-class areas, though in the 19ᵉ things are
changing. There, straddling the Canal de l'Ourcq on the site of
the old abattoirs, is the brand-new Parc de la Villette
containing a spacious exhibition hall, the Zenith venue for rock
concerts, the extraordinary hemispherical Géode cinema and
next door the enormous hi-tech museum of the future, La Cité
des Sciences et de l'Industrie. Within a few years this is likely to
become one of Paris's greatest attractions, and the effects on
the local community and economy will be dramatic. Already
the canal at the Bassin de la Villette (the extension of the Canal

Saint-Martin from the 10ᵉ), formerly an industrial warehousing area for canal-borne goods (backdrop for the film *Diva*, incidentally), has been tidied up in preparation for its new leisure role, and luxury flats with a view of the water are springing up all around. One of the few original features still remaining is the century-old Pont de Crimée, the city's last hydraulically-operated drawbridge.

Near by is a park of a different character, the unexpectedly pretty acres of Buttes Chaumont with its artificial lake, cascades and crags. Best approached from the south, it spreads below you like a green, wooded oasis in the urban monotony. A hidden gem.

Moving south into the 20ᵉ there's the 'village' of Belleville, possibly the city's most heterogeneous immigrant area where Greeks, Poles, Russian Jews, Yugoslavs, Portuguese, Spaniards, Armenians, north Africans and many more have found sanctuary during the last hundred years or so. South-east Asians too have added to the mix, and if your taste is for Chinese food (we don't include Chinese in our selection – see the Introduction, p. 28) then the Rue de Belleville is the place to come. Of the many restaurants here, Tai Yien and Empire de Belleville are the most celebrated.

At the heart of the 20ᵉ is the famous Père Lachaise cemetery, whose silent occupants include Oscar Wilde, Modigliani, Colette, Sarah Bernhardt, Proust, Chopin, Edith Piaf, Molière, Delacroix, Apollinaire, Victor Hugo and the doomed lovers Héloïse and Abélard. But the man who has made most impact on Père Lachaise is a more recent arrival – the Doors' singer Jim Morrison, whose grave is permanently surrounded by zomboid adherents to the Morrison cult, silent, adoring pilgrims who've daubed the tombs for yards around with words from his songs and messages of hope for his second coming. Quite bizarre. And up in the north-east corner, don't miss the row of stone memorials to all those who died for political causes – the Communards, the French members of the International Brigades in Spain, the Resistance fighters of the Nazi Occupation and, of course, those murdered in the concentration camps.

Between Père Lachaise and the Boulevard Davout lies the old village of Charonne, which still maintains some of its charm, particularly around the church of Saint-Germain-de-Charonne, with its tiny churchyard, the Rue Stendhal and the Rue Saint-Blaise. And right out at the Porte de Montreuil is one of the city's best flea-markets (Saturday, Sunday and Monday each week) for those who want a good bargain.

BUDGET

Mère-Grand   **Map ref: 20A**
20 Rue Orfila (Mᵒ *Gambetta*)
Tel: 46.36.03.29
Open: lunch and dinner until 20.30
Closed: Sunday
Set menus: 42F, 58F, wine or beer and service included
Wine: 10–12F (50cl)

Close to Père Lachaise cemetery, this neat, lace-curtained
restaurant with a lovely bulging grandfather clock in the corner
is perfect for a cheap, substantial lunch. But it's very popular so
get in before 12.30, by which time groups of more than two
have to wait for a table. There are two set menus, both
including wine or beer and service. The 42F menu offers the
usual range of entrées followed by *steak grillé*, *andouillette*,
poule au pot (chicken casserole) or *langue de bœuf en sauce
gribiche* (beef tongue in mayonnaise with capers and herbs).
For another 16F you can take your pick of *tournedos*, *gigot
d'agneau*, *pintade à la basquaise* and *lapin à la moutarde*. The
last was delicious – an enormous, tender rabbit leg, meat falling
from the bone, in a mild mustard and bacon sauce, and served
with small, perfectly sautéed potatoes – as were most of the
dishes that day.

Finishing off with a slice of delightful *tarte pêches*, the 58F
bill seemed a small price to pay. There's little more to say,
except that this is a wonderful example of the French tradition
of family-run eating-places that we so lack in Britain – good,
fresh-cooked food, served impeccably and presented with style
and care. Catch it while you can – even in France it's a dying
breed.

MODERATE

Incari   **Map ref: 19A**
117 Rue de Meaux (Mᵒ *Laumière*)
Tel: 42.45.83.99
Open: lunch and dinner until 23.00
Closed: Saturday lunch, Sunday lunch
À la carte: 80–100F
Wine: 10F (50cl)
Service: 15%

Well out of the geographical and culinary mainstream, this tiny South American place is a great find and well worth the trip for a good evening out. Run by a large bearded Chilean exile, its small room is graced by a discreet collection of South American artefacts and even more discreet taped music – so don't expect to be dancing the tango on the tables. *Entradas* include *empanadas*, *gallega* (fish tart) and a tempting-looking spinach tart, alongside a refreshing range of *ensaladas*.

Perhaps most interesting are the main dishes, however. The *feijoada*, for example, is superb – pieces of tender pork, beef and sausage cooked in a spicy pepper and tomato sauce, served with rice, black beans and manioc. And besides the inevitable *churrasco* and *chilli con carne* (served without rice) are lesser-known specialities such as *mole de cerdo* (pork cooked with tomatoes and chocolate!) and trout cooked with either orange sauce or nuts. To accompany all this there's a range of Latin American wines by the bottle, mainly hearty reds.

Desserts too are inventive – the *flan à la noix de coco* (a caramel custard on a desiccated coconut base) is a delicious variation of the traditional French flan with a popular Latin American ingredient. Coconut figures amongst the ice-cream flavours too, while papaya and mango can be had in the flesh, so to speak. Three courses of this interesting and unusual cuisine, with half a bottle of wine, will cost you no more than 100F.

La Lumière de Belleville   Map ref: 20B

102 Boulevard de Belleville (Mᵒ *Couronnes* or *Belleville*)
Tel: 47.97.51.83
Open: lunch and dinner until midnight
Closed: Friday dinner, Saturday
À la carte: 100–120F
Wine: 32F (bottle)
Service: 15%

The Belleville area in the north-east of Paris is the home of several immigrant communities, including Chinese, north Africans and Jews. In this lively, relaxed and friendly restaurant, two of these traditions come together – here you'll taste genuine Jewish-Tunisian cuisine and drink kosher wine. The big problem for a reviewer is the wide range of the menu and the strangeness of its contents. The *couscous* range runs to three types plus the *royale*, which is served with lamb, *merguez* and beef, slightly thin on the vegetables but with a tasty sprinkling of sultanas in the *couscous* grain itself. A bottle of the house red or rosé, depending on time of year, complements it perfectly.

If you decide to step off the well-worn *couscous* trail, you're almost on your own, but it'll certainly be a culinary adventure. On the more mundane side there is a range of meat *grillades* and *brochettes*; more interestingly there are several *poisson complet* dishes, including grey mullet, tuna and *rougets* (small red mullet); then there is a series of Jewish-Tunisian specialities such as *akaud* (*tripes tunisienes*), *pkaila* (a spinach-based dish) and *kemia* (minced beef and onion). Finishing off with a sticky north-African pastry – *ananas à la menthe* (pineapple with mint) or *ananas frites* (hot, fried pineapple) – and possibly a glass of the fiery fig liquer, *boukha*, the bill shouldn't come to more than 110–120F, and with care could be much less. For an exotic excursion like this, that is a small price indeed.

Au Rendezvous de la Marine   **Map ref: 19B**
14 Quai de la Loire (Mᵒ *Jaurès*)
Tel: 42.49.33.40
Open: lunch and dinner until 21.30
Closed: Saturday, Sunday
À la carte: 70–90F
Wine: 17F (litre), 25F (bottle)
Service: included

The Bassin de la Villette is little known by foreign tourists, but now that it's being de-industrialized, and the old wharfs and waterway turned into a leisure area, it's bound to get more and more popular. This charming little restaurant, at the south-western end of the Bassin, is excellently situated to start or finish your exploration of the area and perhaps even a walk up the canal to the new Cité des Sciences et de l'Industrie.

As the restaurant's name suggests, it used to be frequented by the bargemen on their way from the Seine up the Canal Saint-Martin and the Canal de l'Ourcq to the Marne Valley. Nowadays it has a more heterogeneous clientele, though gestures towards its past linger on in the form of various nautical objects on the walls over the bar. The atmosphere is lively and friendly, with many a vase of plastic flowers and quaint flock-floral wallpaper. There's no set menu, but prices are very reasonable and the cuisine surprisingly accomplished. Entrées are fairly standard, though well-presented: *charcuterie*, herring, *poireaux vinaigrette*, *frisée aux lardons* and a sharp, peppery *champignons à la grecque*.

Main courses include several fish dishes (as one might expect) – *coquilles Saint-Jacques*, *filet de daurade*, *sole pochée à l'oseille* and *rougets grillés*. You can also order a well-respected *bouillabaisse*, for four, forty-eight hours in advance. Then there is a range of meats – *filet de bœuf au poivre vert*, *côtes d'agneau*, and *magret* and *confit de canard*. The *escalope de veau normande* is especially recommended – a small, tender fillet of veal cooked in a rich sauce of cream, apple and mushrooms and served with perfectly sautéed potatoes. Very unexpected.

Desserts too are varied, with *profiteroles*, *tarte maison* and *crème caramel à l'orange* to the fore, but best bets are the three special ice-cream concoctions laced with liqueur. '*Le Cerisier*' was wonderful – cherry-flavoured ice-cream with real cherries and lashings of *cerise eau de vie*. A beautiful, head-spinning summer dessert. With a small *pichet* of dry white wine and a coffee, three satisfying courses came to around 85F (in the evening you might spend 100F). This is a good rendezvous for anybody.

DELUXE

Chez Combet   Map ref: 20C
10 Rue des Montibœufs (Mᵒ *Porte de Bagnolet*)
Tel: 43.61.09.28
Open: lunch and dinner until 21.30
Closed: Wednesday dinner, Thursday
Set menu: 72F, wine and service included
À la carte: 130–160F, service at 15%
Wine: 25–35F (bottle)
Credit cards: Visa

In the unlikeliest street, tucked away amongst apartment blocks, is this small family-run restaurant. As you wend your way here you'll be wondering why on earth we've dragged you so far from your favourite watering-holes, but the reason will be clear as soon as your food arrives.

As you step inside this small dining-room you'll be greeted by the *patronne*, Christianne Planche, a large, garrulous woman who used to work here under a former *patron* as a waitress; biding her time, she bought the restaurant and its recipes from the owner's family when he died, and now runs the place herself with the help of her irritable daughter. In other, more fashionable establishments you'd pay extra for this kind of ill-tempered family cabaret – here it comes gratis Fortunately, the bickering between mother and daughter never reaches the embarrassment threshold, but if this is what French family life is all about, no wonder it's on the wane!

The menu is traditional and quantities are copious. Starters include *crudités*, *hareng*, *salade niçoise* and *maquereaux au vin blanc* which comes with a potato salad. For main courses there are traditional meat dishes and a good fish menu which includes favourites like *truite amande*, *sole meunière*, *raie au beurre noisette* and daily specials such as fresh salmon and crab served with mayonnaise. But their *tour de force* is *coquilles Saint-Jacques à la provençale*. All too often *provençale* sauces are so heavily laced with garlic that it crowds out the flavour of the other ingredients, but not here: the sauce was light yet distinctive, and a perfect foil for the delicately flavoured *coquilles*. Meat dishes are also good here, especially the *gigot d'agneau* served with *pommes gratin dauphinois* (deep-fried cheesy potatoes).

We rounded off our meal with some delicious *profiteroles* (ice-cold and topped with a hot chocolate sauce) and a particularly good *parfait liègois* (coffee ice-cream, chocolate sauce and copious amounts of Chantilly cream). With a bottle of Muscadet and coffee, our bill came to 310F for two – not cheap, but worth it. You can eat for much less by selecting from the set menu at 72F. If you do this we recommend the dishes with sauces, since the chef seems particularly accomplished in this department. As we left Christianne and her daughter were still rowing, much to the amusement of their clients. A great place!

THE BEST OF THE REST

Food-shops

Ganachaud, 150 Rue Ménilmontant, 20ᵉ (Mᵒ *Pelleport*) – a great bread-shop and *pâtisserie*, offering thirty different shapes and types, including black rye bread and amazing *croissants*. And while you're up in this neck of the woods, take a look at the extraordinary Disney-like housing-estate almost next door (140 Rue Ménilmontant) with its curious turrets and gateways.

Further Reading

We have found the following books both useful and informative and would recommend them for further reading:

The Dumont Guide: Paris and the Île de France (Webb & Bower, 1985) – the best-written and most comprehensive historical and architectural guide to Paris that we have come across.

Edible France: a Travellers' Guide, Glynn Christian (Ebury Press, 1986) – a useful region-by-region guide to French cuisines and specialities.

Food-lovers' Guide to Paris, Patricia Wells (Methuen, 1985) – an attractive, detailed and beautifully produced guide to all aspects of food in Paris. However, it is written by an American, obviously for an affluent audience, so many of her recommendations are very expensive. And she really doesn't stray off the well-beaten track of the inner, more fashionable areas.

Le Guide du Routard: Paris, Pierre Josse and Philippe Gloaguen (Hachette, 1985) – a great down-market guide (in French) to all aspects of Paris. On food a general bias towards the old-fashioned and the very, very meaty.

Paris Walks, Alison and Sonia Landes (Robson Books, 1986) – limited in scope (only five small central areas covered) but well-researched, with a wealth of detailed history and lively anecdotes, plus some tips on shopping and services.

Paupers' Paris, Miles Turner (Pan, 1986) – a low-budget guide with some extremely eccentric opinions (he manages to dismiss the Tour Eiffel and the Champ-de-Mars!). On eating, price is his main criterion, and several of his recommendations are distinctly suspect.

The Rough Guide to France, Baillie, Fisher and Ellingham (Routledge, 1985) – a good general guide to France but, like the rest of the *Rough Guide* series, absolutely hopeless on food.

FURTHER READING

Simple French Food, Richard Olney (Penguin, 1983) – for those who want to have a go themselves when they return home, this is the best French cookery book for the simpler kind of dishes we talk about in this guide. Unfortunately, some of our best-loved classics are not included.

Indexes

INDEX OF
FRENCH CULINARY TERMS

The following is a selective index of terms commonly encountered in French restaurants or on menus. We have omitted words which are in general use in English, such as consommé, and others very close to the English, such as *celeri* and *bifteck*.

à point, medium rare
addition, bill
affiné, refined, matured
agneau, lamb
aiglefin, haddock
aigre-doux, sweet and sour
aiguillettes, thin slivers of duck breast
ail, garlic
aile, wing of poultry or game
aïoli, a blend of olive oil, eggs and garlic
aligot, mashed potatoes with Cantal cheese
aloyau, sirloin of beef
amande, almond
ananas, pineapple
anchoïade, purée of anchovies, olive oil and vinegar
anchois, anchovy
ancienne, à l', in the old style
andouille, cold, smoked sausage
andouillette, small smoked sausage, usually grilled
aneth, dill
anguille, eel
arachide, peanut
araignée de mer, spider crab
asperge, asparagus
assiette, plate
auvergnat, Auvergne-style, often with cabbage, sausage and bacon
avocat, avocado

baba au rhum, sponge cake with rum-flavoured spirit
baguette, long crusty loaf
baies roses, pink peppercorns
ballotine, usually poultry rolled, boned and stuffed

bar, Mediterranean fish, similar to striped bass

barbue, Mediterranean flatfish, like a turbot

basilic, basil

basquaise, Basque-style usually with ham, tomatoes or peppers

bavaroise, cold dessert made with custard and cream

bavette, skirt steak

béarnaise, tarragon-flavoured sauce of egg-yolks, butter, shallots, white wine, vinegar and herbs

Béchamel, white sauce made with flour and butter

beignet, small doughnut

Bercy, thick creamy fish-stock, with wine and onions

betterave, beetroot

beurre noir, sauce of browned butter

bien cuit, well done

bisque, a shellfish soup

blanquette, veal, lamb, chicken or sea-food with egg-and-cream white sauce

blette, Swiss chard

blinis, small, thick pancakes (Jewish)

bœuf au gros sel, boiled beef served with vegetables and coarse salt

boissons comprises, drinks included

bonne-femme, home-style cooking

bordelaise, in the Bordeaux style, often in a sauce of red wine, shallots and bone marrow

boudin, a sausage (often a blood sausage)

bouillabaisse, a substantial Mediterranean fish soup

bouillon, a light broth

boulettes, meatballs

bourguignonne, *à la*, a dish cooked in red wine, onions, mushrooms and bacon

bourride, fish soup

brandade, warm garlicky purée of salt cod

bretonne, Brittany style, often with white beans or with a white wine sauce with carrots, leeks and celery

brioche, rich bread dough

brochet, pike

brochette, kebab

brûlé, caramelized

Cabecou, small, round goat's cheese

cabillaud, fresh cod

cacahuète, peanut

Caen, *à la mode de*, cooked in Calvados or cider

café crème, coffee with milk (more common than *café au lait*) *café liègeois*, originally iced coffee with cream, now a dessert incorporating coffee or chocolate ice-cream and cream

cagouille, a species of small snail

caille, quail

calmar, squid

campagne, à la, country-style

canard, duck

canard de Barbarie, strong-flavoured breed of duck raised in the south-west

canard sauvage, wild duck

caneton, young male duck

cannelle, cinnamon

canette, duckling

capre, caper

carafe d'eau, pitcher of water

carré (d'agneau, de porc, etc.), rack or loin (of lamb, pork, etc.)

Cassis, blackcurrant or blackcurrant liqueur

cassolette, a dish presented in a small casserole

cassoulet, classic casserole of white beans, sausage, goose, duck or other meats

caviar d'aubergine, aubergine purée

cèpe, large wild mushroom

cerfeuil, chervil

cerise, cherry

cervelas, garlicky pork sausage

cervelle, brain, of calf or lamb

champignon, mushroom

champignons à la grecque, mushrooms served cold in a spicy sauce

Chantilly, sweetened whipped cream

chapon, capon (castrated chicken)

charcuterie, cold processed meats, sausages, terrines, pâtés, etc.

charlotte, moulded dessert with custard filling

châteaubriant, thick fillet steak, usually served with a sauce of white wine, beef stock and shallots

chèvre, fromage de, goat's cheese

chipiron, Basque name for a small squid

choix, au, a choice of offerings on the menu

chou, cabbage

choucroute, Alsatian sauerkraut, usually served with sausage, bacon and pork

chou-fleur, cauliflower

ciboulette, chives

citron, lemon

citron vert, lime

civet, stew of game, thickened with blood

clafouti, custard-tart with cherries

claire, type of oyster

cochon (*de lait*), pig (suckling)

cochonnailles, pork products, usually assorted sausages or pâtés

colin, hake

compote, stewed fresh or dried fruit

concombre, cucumber

confit, usually duck or goose, cooked and preserved in its own fat

coq (*au vin*), chicken (in a red wine sauce)

coquelet, young male chicken

coquilles Saint-Jacques, sea scallops

corbeille (*de fruits*), basket (of fruits)

cornichon, tiny pickle, often gherkin

côte (*d'agneau*, *de porc*), (lamb) chop

coulis, purée of vegetables or fruit

coupe, a cup, a dessert served in a goblet

court bouillon, aromatic broth, common for cooking fish in Antillean cuisine

couscous, granules of semolina or wheat-flour; the whole North African dish with meat and vegetable broth

couteau, knife

couvert, place-setting

crème anglaise, a custard sauce

crème brûlée/crème caramel, rich custard sauce topped with caramelized sugar

crème fraîche, thick, unsweetened cream

crêpe, thin pancake

cresson, watercress

crevette, shrimp

croque-monsieur, toasted ham and cheese sandwich

crottin (*de Chavignol*), firm goat's cheese, often served hot (*chaud*) on toast

croûte, *en*, in pastry

croûtons, small cubes of toasted or fried bread

cru, raw

crudités, raw vegetables

cuisse, leg of poultry

cuit, cooked

darne, fish-steak, most often salmon

daube, stew, usually meat
daurade, type of fish like a sea-bream
dégustation, tasting or sampling
déjeuner, lunch
délice, a type of dessert
demi, half, but of beer refers to a quarter litre (25cl)
dijonnaise, Dijon style, usually incorporating mustard
dinde, turkey-hen
dindon, young turkey
doux/douce, sweet

échalotes, shallots (small onions)
elingus, a hake-like fish
émincé, thin slice, usually meat
encornet, small squid
entrecôte, beef rib steak
entrée, first course
épaule, shoulder (of pork, lamb, etc.)
éperlan, fried whitebait
épice, spice
épinard, spinach
équille, sand eel
escargot, snail
estouffade, stew
estragon, tarragon

façon de, à la, in the fashion of
faisan, pheasant
farci, stuffed
faux-filet, sirloin steak
fenouil, fennel
feuilletage, en/feuilleté, in puff pastry
figue, fig
flageolets, small white-green kidney-beans
flambé, flamed
flan, sweet or savoury tart/custard-pie
foie, liver
foie gras, fattened liver of duck or goose
fondu, melted
forestière, garnish of bacon, wild mushrooms and potatoes
four, au, baked in the oven
fourchette, fork
fraise, strawberry
framboise, raspberry
fricassée, dish consisting of stewed or sautéed ingredients

frisée, curly, as in curly endives
frites, (*pommes*), french fries
friture, a fried dish
fromage blanc, a smooth cheese similar to cottage-cheese
fromage de tête, 'head cheese', similar to brawn
fruits de mer, sea-food
fumé, smoked

galette, savoury pancake, usually served as entrée or main
   course
garni, garnished
gêsier, gizzard
gigot, usually leg of lamb
gingembre, ginger
glace, ice-cream
glacé, iced, glazed or crystallized
goujons, small fish, generally breadcrumbed and deep-fried
graine de moutarde, mustard-seed
gratin, baked crusty-topped dish or casserole
gratin dauphinois, baked casserole of potatoes, cheese and
   milk
gratiné, having a crusty, brown top
grenouilles, *cuisses de*, frogs' legs
grillade, grilled meat
groseille, red-currant

hareng, herring
haricot, bean
haricot rouge, red kidney-bean
homard, lobster
huile, oil
huître, oyster

île flottante, a dessert of soft meringue in crème anglaise,
   usually topped with caramel. Used interchangeably with
   œufs à la neige
indienne, *à l'*, (usually) curried
infusion, herb tea

jambon, ham
jambonneau, pork knuckle
jaret de veau, a veal stew
jus, juice

kir, an aperitif of dry white wine and Crème de Cassis

kougelhopf, sweet Alsatian bread-cake, with almonds and
  raisins

langouste, crawfish, a type of lobster
langoustine, small lobster
langue, tongue
lapereau, young rabbit
lapin, rabbit
lard, bacon
lardon, cube of bacon (as in *frisée aux lardons*)
légume, vegetable
lièvre, hare
lotte, monkfish
lyonnaise, à la, in the style of Lyons, usually garnished with
  onions

macédoine, diced mixture of vegetables or fruit
madeleines, small tea-cakes
magret de canard (d'oie), breast of fattened duck (goose)
maïs, corn
mange-tout, a green runner-bean
mangue, mango
maquereau, mackerel
marron, chestnut
médaillon, round piece or slice (of meat, fish)
mélange, mixture
menthe, mint
merguez, small spicy sausage
merlan, whiting
merle, blackbird
meunière, à la, (fish) rolled in flour and cooked in butter
miel, honey
mille-feuille, puff-pastry
mimosa, garnish of chopped, hard-boiled egg-yolks
moelle, beef bone marrow
morceau, piece
morille, morel (a kind of wild mushroom)
morue, salted or dried cod
moule, mussel
moules marinière, mussels cooked in white wine with onions
  and herbs
mousseline, ingredients whipped with cream or egg-whites to
  lighten them, as in sauces
mouton, mutton
muscade, nutmeg

museau de porc (*bœuf*), muzzle of pork (beef)
myrtilles, bilberries
mystère, an ice-cream dessert, sometimes with meringue and
    chocolate

navet, turnip
noisette, hazelnut, or also the centre cut of lamb
noix, walnut or simply nut, as in *noix de coco*
normande, in the style of Normandy: (i) with cream and
    mushrooms; or (ii) cooked in cider or Calvados
nouilles, noodles

œuf, egg
œufs à la neige, see *île flottante*
oie, goose
oignon, onion
onglet, beef flank steak
oseille, sorrel
oursin, spiny sea-urchin

palmier, sugared puff-pastry biscuit
pamplemousse, grapefruit
panaché, mixture or mixed
pané, breaded
papillote, *en*, cooked in a foil wrapping
parfait, a type of mousse
parmentier, dish with potatoes
pâte, pastry or dough
pâté, moulded, spiced mince-meat
pâtes (*fraîches*), pasta (fresh)
paupiette, thin slice of meat
pavé, thick slice of beef
paysanne, *à la*, country style, usually with simple vegetables
    and bacon
persil, parsley
pied (*de porc, veau*), foot (of pig, veal)
pigeonneau, squab (young pigeon)
pintade, guinea-fowl
pintadeau, baby guinea-fowl
piperade, Basque dish containing egg, tomatoes, onions,
    peppers and ham
pissaladière, a kind of savoury flan
pistou, a basil sauce
pithiviers, a puff-pastry full of almond-cream

plateau de fruits de mer, enormous platter of a wide range of raw and cooked shellfish and sea-food

poché, poached

poêlé, pan-fried

poire, pear

poireau, leek

pois, pea

poisson, fish

poitrine, breast of meat or poultry

poivre, pepper (or peppercorns as in *poivre rose/noir/vert*)

pomme, apple

pomme de terre, potato

pommes frites, french fries

potage, soup

pot-au-feu, a hearty boiled beef and vegetable stew

potée, hearty soup of pork and vegetables

poularde, fatted hen

poulet, chicken

poulet basquaise, Basque-style chicken, with peppers and tomatoes

poulpe, octopus

poussin, baby chicken

prix fixe, fixed-price menu

prix net, service included

provençal, in the style of Provence, with garlic, tomatoes and olive oil

prune, fresh plum

pruneau, prune

quenelle, a fish or poultry dumpling

raclette, Swiss dish of melted cheese on boiled potatoes

ragoût, stew, usually with meat

raie, skate-fish

raisin, grape

rascasse, hogfish

ravigote, usually a thick vinaigrette sauce

rémoulade, sauce of mayonnaise, capers, mustard, herbs and anchovies

rillettes/rillons, a coarsely-minced pâté (of duck, pork, etc)

ris (*d'agneau, de veau*, etc.), sweetbreads (thymus) (of lamb, veal, etc.)

riz, rice

rognons, kidneys

rôti, roast

rougail, a highly spiced purée
rouget, red mullet
roulé, rolled
roussette, dogfish

saignant, very rare (of meat)
Saint-Jacques, coquilles, sea scallops
salé, salted, pickled
saucisse, small fresh sausage
saucisson, large dried sausage
saumon, salmon
sauté, browned in fat
sel, salt
service en sus, service not included
sorbet, a kind of light, flavoured water-ice
sucre, sugar

tartare, chopped raw beef, usually with raw egg
tarte tatin, caramelized, upside-down apple tart
tartine, open sandwich or simply buttered bread
tête de veau (porc), head of veal (pork), incorporating brain
   and tongue
thé, tea
thon, tuna
tortue, turtle
tournedos, fillet of beef
tourteau, large crab
tripes à la (mode de) Caen, tripe cooked in Calvados
tripoux, mutton-tripe
truite, trout

vacherin, dessert of meringue, ice-cream and cream
vapeur (à la), steamed
veau, veal
viande, meat
Vichy, generic term for mineral-water
vichyssoise, cold, creamy leek and potato soup
volaille, poultry
volonté, à, at the customer's discretion

Xérès, sherry

yaourt, yoghurt

ALPHABETICAL INDEX
OF RESTAURANTS

Each restaurant in the following indexes is accompanied by a reference to the maps at the front of the book (pp. 8–11). The number indicates the *arrondissement* in which the restaurant can be found.

INDEX OF RESTAURANTS
SPECIALIZING IN FISH

INDEX OF RESTAURANTS
SERVING VEGETARIAN DISHES

INDEX OF RESTAURANTS
SERVING NON-FRENCH CUISINE

INDEX OF
LATE-CLOSING RESTAURANTS

This is a list of restaurants that stay open regularly after 22.30.
However, in slack periods or in winter they may close earlier
than advertised. Conversely, others not listed here may at
times stay open late.

INDEX OF RESTAURANTS
OPEN ON SUNDAYS

INDEX OF
THE BEST OF THE REST
Wine-bars – cafés – bars

Salons de thé

Food-shops